SEAN FEUCHT

BRAZEN

Be A Voice, Not An Echo

Cover Design by Whitney Whitt
Cover Photography by Rachel Soh
Interior Design by Allan Nygren

N|T NEWTYPE

Published by NEWTYPE Publishing
newtypepublishing.com
Paperback ISBN: 978-1-952421-07-5
eISBN: 978-1-952421-08-2

First Edition

Printed in the United States.

To my high school girlfriend, the mother of my four
children and my beautiful bride for the last 15 years:
thank you for standing beside me on the wild journey.
You are by far God's greatest gift to my life.

CONTENTS

FOREWORD

The moment I heard about this long-haired worship leader from California who was taking a bold stand to run for US Congress, my heart leapt with excitement. I knew that regardless of the outcome, this young, energetic leader would provide a wave of fresh perspective in a political arena that is experiencing the greatest battle of our time, one that will determine the future of our nation.

There are several reasons Sean struck me as a candidate worth endorsing, not least of which was his faith in God. I've been a man of faith for as long as I can remember, and it is my faith that informs everything I set my hands to—ministry, politics, music, supporting my family. I see that very same value in Sean.

In many ways, our journeys share some incredible similarities. As worship leaders and preachers, we were both first called to serve the body of Christ through traditional ministry. Sean through worship, prayer, and missions; me through pastoral and denominational leadership. And then life presented us with detours.

We both made the leap from ministry to politics at a young age. In fact, my first step into the political arena was a campaign for Senate when I was close to Sean's age. What then felt like a huge misstep (I didn't win) turned out to be God's hand on my life. I found myself in a position to serve my state as lieutenant governor, and eventually as the 44th governor of Arkansas.

But why would God take a worship leader and missionary, or a Baptist pastor, and compel him to run for political office? Why detour his life so profoundly?

God has a way of creating opportunity from adversity and leading us toward the outcome that is His will, rather than the goal or dream that is ours. I have experienced this in my own life, and I can see it clearly in Sean's as well.

Detours are those moments when we're confident that we're going in the right direction, God is even leading us in that direction, and then suddenly we're taken off our path. I have had a lot of detours in my life—the shift from ministry to politics, my presidential campaigns—those moments when I was heading in one direction and God guided me (sometimes quite suddenly) in another.

We have all experienced detours: broken dreams, broken hearts, hope deferred. We don't plan for them. We don't often like them—except perhaps in retrospect. And we especially do not celebrate them. But the truth is, sometimes the detour leads to a far better destination than anything we can ever plan.

Romans 8:28 says, "And we know that in all things God works for the good of those who love him, who have been called according to his purpose."

The Word of God is clear. Even when we think we are facing the worst of circumstances in life, God can transform it into something profoundly good.

He is so much bigger than our circumstances, problems, and pain. And when we begin to embrace that truth, and embrace the detours, we begin to see life from God's perspective. We begin to live in radical—or brazen—faith.

Sean's life story is full of detours; unexpected changes in course, career, and even calling. Yet, as his journey testifies, by choosing a life that puts trust and faith in God above all else, you will see things you never would have seen, and go places you never would have gone.

Like so many of us, he faced life's detours with questions: God, is this You? Am I on the right path? But he did so while also demonstrating a profound focus on the Person of Christ, the One whose voice matters most of all. And the Lord was always faithful to answer, continually guiding Sean toward a destination he couldn't yet see.

I know full well the challenges we face when attempting to pursue the calling of God on our lives, especially when following His leading into the political world. It is not always easy to pursue the unknown and let His voice drown out the noise that surrounds us.

I believe this book, and Sean's story of radical faith, will be a source of inspiration to a generation of worshipers. His pursuit of God's calling on His life is an invitation for others to wholeheartedly chase God's will and purposes on the earth.

We as a culture have lost focus and are no longer in tune with any standard, be it moral, spiritual, or otherwise. We are only in tune with what we want, the plans that we have for ourselves. This selfish approach to life is devastating our society and our nation.

Now, more than ever, we need brazen, faith-filled leaders to stand up and speak out. We need a generation of leaders who will boldly pursue much-desired change in our nation. We need those who will be willingly detoured from their own plans in order to fulfill God's great plans for this world.

I was so proud to have the opportunity to endorse Sean's political campaign and I am excited to see where God leads him in these trying days. Let his words and his story transform you and draw you into a deeper passion for God. It is time for us, as a nation, to stand up and live with brazen faith!

Mike Huckabee
Former Governor of Arkansas
Two-time Presidential Candidate

"OUTSIDE THE WILL OF GOD, THERE IS NOTHING I WANT. AND IN THE WILL OF GOD, THERE IS NOTHING I FEAR."

A. W. TOZER

SUPER TUESDAY

I'll never forget that day.

I woke up that morning after a rough night's sleep. I am normally a very lighthearted, optimistic guy, but I felt knots in my stomach the second I got out of bed. I couldn't shake the anxiety and nervous tension—*what would this day hold?* I had heard from past candidates that there is a certain finality surrounding elections that is hard to explain. After eight months of pouring my heart, soul, and guts into something so demanding and so intense, I had arrived at the moment of truth. I abandoned so many other pursuits and this was my moment to see if it was all worth it. This was my payday.

I downed three shots of espresso over ice and then called my buddy, Aamon, who was running my campaign. He had moved his entire family across the country from Oklahoma to California a few months prior in response to a crazy word from God and to help me win a seat in the US Congress. Aamon was the direct answer to prayer. I had thrown out a fleece before the Lord, asking God to provide a high-caliber, big-thinking boss to guide this campaign if we had any shot at winning. God answered my prayer through a random meeting—one of my friends met Aamon in a hot tub at a resort. He works in mysterious ways, I guess!

Aamon had just finished helping get the governor of Oklahoma elected (which was another crazy miracle) and running my campaign was the next mountain of victory he felt called to climb. As soon as he arrived in California, we began running a thousand miles an hour.

When I called him that morning, I asked Aamon what his past candidate did on election night to get an idea of what is normal for the day. I felt we would probably need to do something productive and did not want to hold back any energy, resources, or ideas that we could implement before it was all over. I was exhausted, but I was also *all in* and ready to push through to the final moment.

I had never spoken as many times, traveled as much, or raised as much money as I did during that final month. I wanted to leave it all on the field. Despite my anxiety, I woke up ready to fight! I thought there may be some last-minute phone calls we could make, emails to blast, or maybe we could set up signs and a live stream outside a polling station in the center of the district. I was open to anything Aamon felt would be necessary to help secure the victory that night.

He laughed at me on the phone at my perpetually over-eager, "ready to brawl" mindset. He suggested, instead, that we just go fishing. Apparently, California has some pretty strict laws for how close to a polling station you can legally campaign on the day of an election. He also assured me that this particular district was close to 70 percent mail-in ballots, so the election had already been decided a few weeks ago. I was discovering these types of facts—which I never knew—almost every single day.

This was my first ever election, and I looked and sounded like anything but a polished politician. I figured there was virtually no way I would come in first place and beat out the incumbent Democrat. He had held this seat for over ten years. He had also served as the insurance commissioner, lieutenant governor, and was previously in the state assembly. All together, he had been in politics for over forty years and represented some of the most liberal and far left regulations and policies that were crushing the people of the Golden State. Over three thousand people were leaving California every day, and we needed change.

I did feel very confident, though, that as the lone outsider in the race, I could come in second place. That would allow me to continue on to November and build my case to bring a fresh face, a bold voice, and creative solutions to Capitol Hill.

We had raised more money, amassed more social media followers, hosted more campaign events, knocked on more doors, blasted more mailers, and made more calls than any of my Republican competitors. We had an excellent team and we were all working so hard! I had run myself ragged, but I still drew energy from knowing I gave everything I had. That was all that mattered in the end. Besides winning, of course!

My campaign manager assured me to rest in the work we had done. I realized it was all in God's hands now. So we went fishing.

It was a beautiful day of sunshine with no clouds in the sky. We walked across the street from my property to my neighbor's pond and laughed a ton as we reminisced about the crazy things we heard and saw along the campaign trail. Every day we had been floored by how many people were disengaged, did not care, or said the strangest things to us. While we talked, Aamon caught five fish. I caught zero. My mind was way too preoccupied to even focus on casting. I would catch myself staring up into the sky while my line snagged around the bottom of a log.

When we left the pond, I picked up my kids from school, and we made the trip down to our campaign office in downtown Fairfield. On the way down, I fretted to my wife about everything that could potentially go wrong. It is not in my personality at all to fret or worry. Optimism is my only gear and almost everyone who knows me would agree. I always think about the best outcomes.

Yet, there were so many things weighing on my mind in that moment. I worried about a low turnout due to the new virus scare coming from China. The media was already panicking about what would eventually become a global pandemic—COVID-19. Just a few days before Super Tuesday, the first known US case was discovered in the very same district in which I was running. I had a growing fear that many would not show up to the polls due to these concerns. I also knew the relentless fear-mongering of the media was only amplifying the situation. Without a strong turnout from the older generation, millennials, minorities, and independent conservatives, it would be difficult to win.

I also worried about our current momentum. We had an exploding presence online and were getting great press coverage in the national news. But would that translate into local votes inside the district? I was late starting my campaign—did voters know enough about me and my policy positions to take a chance on a long-haired worship leader who did not even live inside the district? We were one of the most watched congressional campaigns in America. I had met with senior officials, congressmen, senators, and even the president and vice president of the United States. Yet, only the voters in CA-3 would determine the outcome.

In the parking lot of Chick-fil-A, a ray of hope came in the form of an African American family. They flagged down our car as we were about to drive away and motioned for me to role down my window. "Are you that Sean guy running for Congress?" they shouted. They were laughing because they recognized me by my hair. Then they pointed to their "I VOTED" stickers on their chests and told me that they had all just voted for me. My kids started cheering and I felt a massive boost of encouragement. With just that small encounter, a surge of confidence shot through my heart and I felt renewed energy as we drove to our watch party.

We pulled into the campaign office right as the polls were beginning to close. We heard a chorus of cheers as a string of people overflowed from our office and almost filled the entire block! Our headquarters was filled with people, finger food, tiny American flags, congress banners, T-shirts, and bottles of champagne waiting to be popped open. There was a distinct energy and excitement as we laughed, waited, smiled, then waited some more.

That was quite possibly the most eclectic crowd of people I had ever seen. Our entire campaign staff was hosting the party, along with our interns, local church leaders, and plenty of random people who had been drawn to our campaign and message along the way. Every single person present had a story of how our lives intersected. They were old, young, Black, white, Hispanic, Asian, and most of them did not even know each other. They were there because they had a reason to believe and fight for change in California.

We set up a room in the very back of the office with a few laptops feeding the live election results onto a large screen out front. My campaign manager was in the back with some of our core team, our wives, and all our kids. Books, toys, blankets, and iPads were scattered around the room to keep them busy while we settled in for the night.

Everyone was wearing "Sean for Congress" T-shirts and smiling proudly with expectation. Our big-screen projection setup was not the smoothest or best looking display, but no one seemed to really mind. I guess it kind of played into our grassroots vibe. We were ready for the watch party to kick into high gear!

This was another first for me. I had never been to a watch party before in my life—I had no idea what to do or how things worked. I kept pacing around the little office and could barely even look at the screen as the first wave of votes rolled in. As the minutes ticked by, however, I began to gain confidence that I would come in second place and move on to November. I did not enter the race only to lose in the primary, especially after building so much momentum and giving it so much of my heart.

After more than a thirty-minute delay—which felt like an eternity—the first numbers came through. I looked over at Aamon as he furiously scoured the New York Times live election results, refreshing the page every ten seconds. The ghastly look on his face as he saw the initial numbers felt like one of the biggest gut punches of my life.

"Okay," he said, "here are the first results! Alright...um...okay...well... so we're starting a little slow here, but thats alright." I looked down at the screen and then immediately did a double take. I couldn't believe what I was seeing! I had to look again. There was dead silence in the room. We were in third place and already behind by thousands of votes. I knew it was just the first update, but I felt deflated.

I had researched enough about congressional elections to know that this was not a good sign at all. Everyone in the room continued to stay optimistic, but I felt like a death decree had already been written. I gave Aamon a fake smile and left the room to walk around the block. No one in the crowded party room had seen the initial results yet, but the numbers would soon be broadcast on the giant screen for all to see.

The night continued to drag on at a snail's pace. The kids were barely awake in the corner of the room and the people were slowly leaving the party one by one as the night wore on. With each update, we fell further and further behind on votes. County by county we watched intently, hoping for a massive turnaround. But it never came.

I was furiously texting my consultants and team in DC who were up late that night tracking our election. They were my mentors, people I had sat with at the RNC headquarters in DC months earlier as they convinced me that *this* was the district. They had emphatically stated that *this* was the right election cycle and that I was the perfect candidate to take a stand in California. They convinced me that I could turn this thing around and mobilize voters in the Church and disengaged millennials who would not normally show up to vote. I believed them with all my heart. I was all in.

Their combined fifty years of experience in everything from presidential, congressional, and senate races informed me on how to run a successful campaign. We worked together every day for months on messaging, approach, and how to define myself as a unique candidate—one who could fight the status quo. They took a big risk mentoring a first-time candidate with no political experience and I trusted them very deeply through the entire process. They were a dream to work with and I felt so fortunate they chose me to mentor. But I took a big risk as well and laid everything on the line—my music, my career, my finances, my family, and my future. Prior to this decision to run for Congress, I was reaching the pinnacle of my life in so many areas.

In that moment, however, failure began to set in. Deep failure and despair. I knew the writing was on the wall. With each crushing update on the vote totals throughout the rest of the night, I had to go out and face the most committed people ever to run a campaign and try to remain hopeful. They had walked hundreds of miles canvassing neighborhoods, held weekly prayer meetings, made tons of phone calls, and believed with everything inside of them that I could win. Most of them had never been involved in a campaign before. Lots of them had never even voted before! They gave everything to the race. And I let them down with false hopes and broken promises.

We finally left the campaign office around midnight to make the three-hour trip home. It felt like the longest and loneliest drive of my entire life. The kids quickly fell asleep and I did not want to talk to my wife or respond to anyone calling or texting. I didn't want to process anything. I completely shut down. I just wanted to escape, to pretend it never happened. I was embarrassed, confused, belittled, and angry. I was angry at so many things—the results, our campaign strategy, at myself for making the stupid decision to put my family and my friends through all of this. Ultimately, I was angry at God. I felt like He let me down. I felt abandoned.

I could not get out of bed the next morning. It was like a ton of bricks were weighing me down. I laid there staring at the ceiling for hours.

This was far more than just a loss (of which I have had many). It felt like a waste of an entire season of my life. I began to question it all from the very beginning. Why did we move to California in the first place? Why did we believe we could jump into politics and change anything? How were we so easily fooled into all of this? Is this the reward for laying everything on the line to follow what we thought was the voice of God?

My whole life I had chased God's heart with bold faith and abandon. But this time, I wondered if it had been faith or foolishness that led me here.

And if it was faith, was it even worth it?

BRAZEN

bra·zen | \ ˈbrā-zᵊn \

adjective

BOLD AND
WITHOUT SHAME

CHAPTER 1

RAINBOW BABY

My parents both grew up in the Deep South. They were the first on both sides of their family to venture out and resettle west of the Mississippi. My dad had always dreamed of living in the mountains. After finishing medical school and residency in Colorado, my parents searched for a town that badly needed another dermatology practice. Missoula, Montana, was that place and they set down roots. Their second child—and first boy—was born in 1982. They named him Christopher after my dad; he was the apple of my dad's eye. Then, the most horrendous and painful tragedy happened not long after Christopher was born. My parents took an overnight trip several hours away from Missoula and they had a babysitter, a close family friend, stay with the kids for the night.

The first night they were gone, Christopher suddenly suffocated and died in his sleep. No one knew or understood why. It could have happened from a crib malfunction—there were other deaths reported by the manufacturer that year. He was just ten weeks old. My parents were completely devastated. It was by far the biggest crisis of their young family. Their beautiful Assemblies of God church surrounded them with comfort, prayers, support, and perspective. They could not have been in a better community as they navigated the most tragic season of their lives.

During the memorial service for baby Christopher, one of the pastors began to prophesy over my parents. He shared that a season of promise was coming when God would restore what was taken. He saw a rainbow in his mind's eye and prayed and declared that it was a sign of what was to come. He spoke of a baby that would bring joy where there was sorrow.

Up until that point, it had always taken a few years for my mom to get pregnant. Yet, one year to the exact day of Christopher's death, I was born. My parents and the entire community believed that the prophecy had been fulfilled and a child of promise had been born. The term "rainbow baby" refers to a baby born subsequent to a miscarriage, stillbirth, or the death of an infant. I was their rainbow baby.

———

Growing up in Montana was the best childhood experience I could have ever been given. We lived on the edge of a neighborhood that butted up to the wild and untamed Rocky Mountains. My parents eventually had two more children, and as the only boy, I found myself seeking adventure in the great outdoors. Not a day went by—even during a negative twenty-five degree blizzard—that I did not roam those mountains. It was all an adventurous boy could want in life: absolute freedom to roam, explore, and discover.

When I was ten, however, my parents made the most radical decision of their lives (next to moving to Montana in the first place). They had been bitten by the bug of world missions and could not shake it. In addition to building and sustaining a thriving dermatology practice, my dad was also pioneering and leading missions teams a few times per year around the world. It started with one trip to Romania, and before long, they were serving many different unreached nations across the globe.

Dad recruited doctors, nurses, friends, and anyone with a heart to help serve the poorest of the poor. This began to consume not only his time but also his heart. It was all he ever wanted to do and the reason he became a doctor.

An organization based at the Christian Broadcasting Network (CBN) headquarters in Virginia Beach, Virginia reached out to my dad with a job offer. They wanted him to help lead and pioneer initiatives within their missions arm, "Operation Blessing." The salary was going to be less than one-fourth of what he made from his medical practice in Montana. But money never mattered to my dad, and he took the job with extreme joy and expectation.

I'll never forget the night, in 1993, when my parents told us we would be moving. They took us to our favorite steakhouse and broke the news to me and my three sisters. My sisters were genuinely excited about the move to the East Coast. I, however, was completely crushed by the news. I had fallen in love with Montana and all I wanted to do was explore, hunt, fish, and live there the rest of my life! But I was only ten years old and had no choice or say in the matter. It was final. I begrudgingly packed up my belongings and left the only town, people, and way of life I had every known. What I didn't realize at the time was how much that decision to pursue God would profoundly affect the entire course of my life (as well as the lives of millions of others).

My dad was so beloved in the community that even the front page of the ` featured a goodbye tribute to him and our family. Not many people in Montana, however, understood where we were going or why. Yet, throughout so many voices, questions, and people exerting their own opinions, my dad followed the only Voice that mattered. He was overjoyed that all of his years in college, medical school, residency, and now building his practice had led him to that moment. But more than that, he was demonstrating what it means to live with boldness. It was there, as a ten-year-old watching my parents navigate life with God, that I first experienced—or observed—brazen faith.

———

I remember that first day in Virginia, stepping outside into sticky, wet summer air that suffocated my lungs. I immediately ran back into the safety of the air-conditioned house. I could barely breathe. It was the first time in my life I had ever experienced humidity and I hated it.

I despised almost everything about Virginia at that point. It was flat. It was hot. We were living in a classic suburban neighborhood. Instead of walking out the door and up the mountains, I would ride my bike down the street to Wendy's and 7-Eleven. There weren't any mountains to hike or dangerous animals to run from. No unadulterated and expansive terrain to navigate and explore. There was also a decided lack of friends.

I thought the whole world was crashing down around me. I tried my best to focus my energy on sports and began playing football and basketball. Despite that, over the next two years, I had a growing desire to return home. I lay awake at night dreaming of going back to Montana. I prayed to God that the job would not work out for my dad. My prayers were not answered. Quite the opposite, actually.

My dad knew how hard the move had been on me and how much I still missed Montana, so he surprised me one day with a plan to go with him on a mission trip. There were some very remote tribes in the interior jungles of Brazil that his organization hoped to reach with medicine, aid, and the gospel of Christ.

It would not be a standard, safe, or predictable experience. The only way to reach these tribes was to take a boat loaded with food, medicine, and doctors up the fingers of the Amazon River. Few people knew where or even if these tribes existed. My dad thought this would be the perfect first trip for me.

As a boy who had only known the white, homogenized community in the mountains of Montana, I would suddenly be exposed to cultures, languages, and tribes I had only ever read about. It was like the story of the missionary Jim Elliot coming to life before my very eyes! Although, I confess, I was slightly apprehensive as well—I certainly didn't want my story to end the way his had ended.

Dad and I flew into Manaus, where I received my very first passport stamp as we passed through customs. It was a surreal moment. We made our way to the river and began loading a large boat with all the supplies and medicine we brought from the States. This would be our home for the next twelve days.

The boat was very rustic, to say the least. The bathroom consisted of a hole leading directly into the river, and the inside of the cabin was sweltering hot during the day. As each doctor, nurse, and team member chose their room on the boat, I opted to sleep under a mosquito net in one of the hammocks hanging on the deck. The nights were so humid that my choice to stay above deck meant I could catch even the slightest breeze off the water. Not only that, but I had the best view of the clearest night sky I had ever seen in my life.

When I first met the Brazilian captain of our boat, he informed me that we did not have refrigerators or any device to chill our food during the journey. I was the youngest and only non-medical member of the team, so he grabbed a fishing pole, put it in my hand, and said, "It's your job to catch us fish that we are going to eat every day." I thought he was kidding. It turned out that he was not.

I fished every morning and every evening like it *was* my job. I caught and ate more exotic fish than I could count. There were massive rainbow bass and large black piranhas with teeth as big as human dentures. We ate them all. Our ship's cook knew exactly how to fry them to perfection.

Every day, we stopped at a new village along the Amazon and set up a medical clinic. I woke up early and fished for our food before the medical clinics started. Then I helped unload the boat and joined the medical team setting up the daily clinic on the river bank. The villagers lined up early in the morning, and canoes streamed in from the surrounding areas loaded down with entire families. Many sick showed up, waiting to be seen by a doctor, dentist, or nurse. For many of the tribal people, that was their first time seeing a foreigner—much less a doctor, dentist, or nurse.

The region was so remote it felt like stepping into one of those wild episodes on National Geographic! My twelve-year-old American brain could hardly comprehend that people around the world still lived in such rough conditions. Not only were the situations dire and the people living in extreme poverty, but they also battled so much sickness and unknown disease.

Yet, the power of God met them there. Before any doctor, nurse, or dentist treated a patient, we prayed over each person one by one as they came through the doors of the clinic. In those moments, I witnessed the wildest miracles of my entire life! Things I had only read about in the Bible and in revival history were taking place in front of my eyes. My belief in the power of God manifested right there in the midst of people's desperate need.

There were too many miracles to count. The most notable was a lady who stumbled into the prayer tent held up by two family members. She was blinded by cataracts. The moment we started praying, I saw the cataracts fall off her eyes like scales. It was unbelievable!

Later, I witnessed a man on a stretcher being carried into the tent by his friends, like the story in Luke 5. When we finished praying for him, he jumped up—*right in front of me*—and started walking around the medical clinic. After that divine miracle, the entire village came to Jesus during the crusade we held later that night!

I also experienced aggressive demonic torment, heaviness, and oppression for the first time on that trip. One day, a little old lady walked into the clinic and began to manifest loudly and openly when we began to pray. Her eyes turned blood red, her voice turned deep like a man's, and she became aggressive with everyone around her. My dad laid hands on her and commanded the demon to leave. I saw immediate relief and peace come over her body and her mind. That moment elevated my dad's status in my mind for the rest of my life. He did not even flinch as he hugged her before moving on to the next patient. I was blown away.

I started to see and experience why my dad felt more alive in this context. Not only was he using his skill of medicine to help people (a skill he had worked hard his entire life to acquire), but God was showing up in the middle of it. Every village we visited, the Holy Spirit continued to move. Each and every day, we experienced something new and fresh and wild and alive. Not only were we able to meet people's physical needs, but they were also hearing about Jesus for the first time! They were giving Him their hearts!

The healed, saved, and joyful tribes lined the banks of the river each night offering gifts to show their love and appreciation for our team. Sometimes they would hold out flowers. Other times they would bring us a canoe full of freshly caught fish! It was the most genuine and powerful display of gratitude I had ever seen. These villagers possessed nothing but the huts that they lived in and the clothes on their backs. Yet, they would even offer us those. They were moved to tears that we would come and give everything without asking for anything in return.

During every moment of expressed gratitude, I felt my heart beating stronger and stronger for the nations. I was beginning to understand why I was created and what I was put here on this earth to do.

Growing up, I was never really into movies, video games, or many of the things my friends enjoyed. I genuinely had no interest in them. Instead, I lived for adventure. I woke up imagining what was over the next mountain, the one I couldn't reach the day before. It never dawned on me until I stood in Brazil that missions and adventure could go hand in hand. My passions collided on that trip. I could cruise through unknown tributaries of the Amazon while catching my own fish to eat, leading entire tribes to Jesus, and experiencing God's power like never before! It was everything I imagined adventure and life to be. That trip redefined missions in my mind and the trajectory of my life changed forever.

I woke up that last day on the river wishing we could keep going on forever. Well, actually, I was pretty tired of eating fish at that point. But everything else could go on forever. I decided I needed to do something radical in order to memorialize that moment. I wanted to take a public stand for Christ with something I had never done before.

I asked my dad if he would baptize me after the clinic that day on the riverbank. I would dedicate my life to the nations. Word quickly spread around the village and among the team about the baptism. What was meant to be a simple and private time with my dad turned into so much more. When the clinic was over that day, we started packing up the boat to head back to Manaus. Suddenly, a large group of villagers appeared, dressed in white gowns.

The gowns they wore held great tribal significance. They represented a new season and a new start for everyone who gave their lives to Jesus. They brought a white gown for me and asked that I wear it as my dad prepared to baptize me. I had no idea anyone even knew of our plan. The team came out and leaned against the rails of the boat while the villagers stood on the bank of the river smiling and laughing. I put the white gown over my clothes and they cheered with delight.

The tribe began to sing a worship song in their native language as my dad and I prayed together. Dad then put me under the water in the Amazon River, and when I surfaced, I felt a profound sense of destiny and calling on my life. The tribe was singing, fish were swimming around my feet, and the Presence of God fell heavily upon me in that moment. It was a truly holy experience. I had become new and everything—and I mean everything—had changed.

———

I returned home from that trip with my heart ablaze for the nations. I no longer cared that we were living in Virginia instead of Montana, and I stopped praying that my dad's job wouldn't work out. I only cared about one thing. I somehow knew with everything in me that I would give my entire life to sharing God's kingdom with the world. It became my focus and my obsession.

I began reading and researching everything about unreached people groups, missionary stories of old, and even revival history. I scoured the local Christian bookstore and discovered DC Talk's book *Voice of the Martyr*. I read the stories of the persecuted Church around the world; they enthralled me. I had always been obsessed with maps, and that passion grew even stronger. I converted one entire wall of my bedroom to hold an enlarged map of the world. I would go to sleep every night memorizing the most remote and distant continents, nations, cities, and people groups that I could find.

As I read and discovered, one article in particular stuck out to me.

It detailed the top five most persecuted nations in the world: North Korea, Saudi Arabia, Iraq, Iran, and Afghanistan. I wrote those five nations down on a sticky note and stuck it to my wall. Then I began studying each nation, the people who lived there, the languages they spoke, and the religions they practiced. Those nations became my mission and purpose.

Every night before I went to bed, I prayed that the doors would open for me to experience God moving in each of those nations. I continued to pray the same prayer each night from that point on. And while I had no idea how or when, I was completely convinced that, one day, my prayers would be answered.

CHAPTER 2

HEART OF WORSHIP

Another major shift that took place when I returned from Brazil was my heart for worship. Something changed as I came out of the water and heard the sound of the tribal leaders singing. I caught something divine that day.

I did not have any musical aspirations at that point in my life. I was still completely engrossed in sports and was training to be a quarterback on my football team and a guard on my basketball team. Sports were my main outlet in life at the time, apart from missions. I also didn't have any history with music—I had never learned an instrument and I didn't take lessons growing up. I didn't even think I had a great voice, but I never let that hold me back from worshiping corporately.

Worship was always my favorite part of a church service, however, and after Brazil, something deeper and new came alive in me. Every time I went to church, youth group, or any other corporate worship gathering, I was the first one up front, pressing in and singing my heart out.

All that really mattered to me was being in that place where God's tangible Presence would come and fill a room. I became obsessed with that sense of God's nearness, the surrender of my soul, and that feeling of expectation and adventure with God.

When my sixteenth birthday was drawing near, my mom began to pry my closest friends in youth group about what gift to get me (as only good moms do!). They told her to get me a guitar because they knew I was really into worship. Almost all of them were musicians and played in the youth group band. They told her that they could teach me a chord or two to get me going.

Around that time, my youth group was launching a new home group that would meet at my house every week. I was leading it along with a friend of mine. Just three weeks after receiving my first guitar, the worship leader for that week cancelled just a few hours before we were set to begin. There was no other option but for me to try to lead worship for the first time ever! I resisted it with everything inside of me, but my youth pastor and friends in leadership convinced me that I should at least give it a shot. I tried my best to explain that all I could offer that night was a whopping three chords! I also only knew three songs.

The night was an absolute train wreck. I continually broke out in a nervous sweat, strained my voice, and broke not just one but two guitar strings! I was embarrassed and ashamed in front of fifteen of my peers. I remember running to my room afterward, vowing that I would never lead worship in public again. I only needed to learn enough guitar to play someday in a hut in China, with people who would not care how I sound or look. I had no other plans than to move, live, and die in the nations!

God, however, had other plans. Despite my embarrassment, I did continue to lead worship at our home group. I suddenly found myself in a leadership role unlike any I had experienced before. I was responsible for creating a plan for worship, a time to share testimonies, a short message, and some sort of takeaway each week. Not only that, but this had to all be done in front of my friends and peers!

After a few months, the group grew from fifteen people to over seventy. My house couldn't comfortably contain the number of people who wanted to come and we started turning people away. I can assure you, people were *not* coming for the worship. Rather, we were at the beginning of an incredible move of God that would sweep through our entire youth group.

———

Just a few months later, the worship leader for our main Wednesday youth gatherings left for college, and his entire band left with him. There was now a gaping hole that we had no immediate options to fill. After watching how much I had progressed in leading the home group, and really not having any other option, the leadership team asked me to lead worship for the entire youth group.

As I drove to sound check that Wednesday, the humid Virginia air was blowing through the car windows and my stomach was in knots—a culmination of anxious expectation and almost certain embarrassment. I knew I was about to do something far out of my league and skill set. *At least I know a full four chords*, I told myself. My playing was rough and I was still self-conscious about my voice, but at least I was progressing.

Somehow, I pushed past the anxious thoughts and a boldness and confidence rose inside me. I carried the full expectation that God would show up like He always did, regardless of my glaring weaknesses and imperfections. If His presence showed up, that is all that mattered.

What unfolded, however, was yet another real-life nightmare. I broke two strings…during the very first song. The drummer and electric guitarist basically played solos while I prayed and sang into the mic. I exhibited a ton of raw passion and very little skill (the other band members did great).

Somehow, though, my youth pastor saw potential in us and encouraged us to try again. The entire youth group suffered for weeks until we started to get the hang of it. Many guitar strings were broken in the process. Yet, the atmosphere of hunger seemed to cover our weaknesses. There was a fire burning in the hearts of our youth group that could not be stopped.

Our youth group began experiencing a profound move of God. We met in a dingy middle school cafeteria with a minimal Peavey sound system and crooked overhead projector. It was a stark contrast to the more hip youth groups in town. Yet, it seemed to fit our grassroots and missional vibe. All that mattered to us was God's presence. Our program was anything but polished, predictable, and pretty. It was actually the total opposite and kind of messy at times. But we could feel the expectation of joy and anticipation that something amazing was about to happen almost every time we gathered. Even our weekly attendance exploded overnight, from 100 to over 400 some weeks.

New kids showed up every week and got saved, delivered, and baptized in the Holy Spirit. As a band, we began writing new songs that we would try out each week. And God really did show up. Most nights went longer than planned and would end with us getting kicked out by the local school janitor. Our hearts would be on fire from that night's encounter and we did not always know what to do with that burning passion. Somehow, we would often find ourselves heading over to the local hospital to pray for people.

Over the years, I had developed some connections with the administrators who ran the local ICU. They would allow our youth group to come into the unit in small group rotations and offer prayer to those in the waiting room. Not one person refused prayer in the ICU. God showed up in many amazing ways and every week we went home with the testimonies of His goodness and a renewed confidence and momentum.

I learned a lot during this season, including the leadership skills of boldness, intensity, and courage. I was willing to try anything, even things that had never been done before. We set up speakers and hosted worship nights outside our local Starbucks every other week. We also hosted several large worship and ministry times on the main stages at the beachfront where thousands would gather and stroll by. At one point, I rallied an avid group of friends to do door-to-door evangelism with me each week. It went really well until we were banned by several of the neighborhood associations, including my own. But we saw many salvations and miracles while it lasted. Something so fresh was taking place in our community in that season!

In the midst of this momentum, a leader of our community introduced us to a burned disc that contained some of the wildest prayers, prophecies, and decrees I had ever heard. When my friends and I listened to it, our hearts began to burn. It somehow gave language and an expression to what we were already feeling—God was calling us to deeper intimacy and greater boldness.

The CD was from a new prayer movement known as TheCall. We didn't know much about it, but we were eager to find out what God was doing across America. The prayers for revival coming out of TheCall were exactly what our hearts longed for. We learned that the next gathering would be held at the National Mall in Washington, DC that coming September. We determined that nothing would keep us from that event.

———

It was also during this season that I met a beautiful girl named Kate. I hadn't dated before and had never really spent much time alone with girls. I wasn't against dating nor was I super legalistic; I simply hadn't met a girl that I wanted to pursue. That is, until Kate came along.

She was the most beautiful thing on planet Earth. Bright blue eyes, sun-kissed skin, blond hair, and the cutest dimple on her left cheek. Her parents were both pastors and had recently moved back to the area after a brief stint in Wisconsin. When I first met Kate, her face was eerily familiar to me. I couldn't seem to place how I knew her, but I knew there was some sort of history between us.

I tried to be low-key with my interest. I would ask people about her, without *really* asking them, trying to figure out who she was and where she was from. These were the days before social media, so the chain of communication depended on that one person who seemed to know everything about everyone. I had a few of those friends and commissioned them to start digging. I could not, for the life of me, remember why her face was so familiar.

Then one day it hit me. She had been on the cheerleading team during my seventh grade basketball season! That's where I remembered that cute dimple and unforgettable smile. She left Virginia after that school year and I never saw her again…until now. What I felt for her was unlike anything I had experienced before, and somehow I just knew we were going to end up together. Her family started going to our church and Kate would come on Wednesday nights to our rowdy youth group meeting in the primary school cafeteria. After several months of fully pursuing her heart, the feelings were reciprocated. She was sixteen and I was seventeen when we started dating. She was the first serious girlfriend I ever had.

I worked hard to convince her parents to send her to my Christian school. She was a grade below me in school, but I really loved seeing her every single day. Kate easily won over every classmate and teacher at our school and was a favorite. She was funny, athletic, grounded, beautiful, smiled all the time, and really loved the Lord. She easily won prom queen her senior year.

What made Kate even more attractive to me, though, was that her heart was turning toward the nations and wanting to do missions. She went on her first overseas mission trip to Europe, which was led by my mom. A few weeks after she returned, I actually went on a mission trip led by her dad to St. Lucia. We connected for life on that trip. He loved sports, adventure, and was a father to four daughters, Kate being the oldest. We connected in deep ways and I knew that he trusted me with his daughter's heart.

———

During that summer, life was very full. My football team was in the middle of three-per-day workouts in 100 degree weather and I was training to become the starting quarterback. When I was not on the field or in the gym, however, I was practicing guitar and mobilizing phone calls to gather people to the event in DC. I was also trying to spend as much time as possible with my new girlfriend. She was going to my small group and I was over at her house almost every night hanging out with her family and playing basketball with her dad in their backyard.

When the day for TheCall DC arrived, no one in our youth group really knew what to expect. We had no preconceived ideas of what it should look like either. We just wanted to be part of whatever God was doing and however He was moving in our nation. We had tasted a little but wanted so much more. Ours was not a church community on the "conference circuit" where itinerate ministers would come speak. Because of that, we really had no context for what was happening outside of our own unique movement.

Our youth group loaded up a few buses and drove down to Washington, DC. Kate and all our friends were part of the group that came. Those first few steps off the charter bus and onto the National Mall in September 2000 were unforgettable. An enormous crowd had gathered from all across America. There was an energy and expectation that was palpable! You could almost feel the electricity of the crowd! This was not a festival; it was a fast. It was the most intense twelve hours of nonstop worship, prayer, and fasting for revival in America I had ever been part of.

There were many well-known church leaders and musicians on stage, but no one had come for the big names, the best songs, or the ministries represented. We were all there for one purpose: to press into and contend for revival and awakening.

Just a few hours into the gathering that morning, over 400,000 people filled every section of the National Mall. Jumbotron screens and massive sound systems were placed every block between the US Capitol Building and the Washington Monument.

It was in that moment that I realized I was not alone. What God had been stirring in our youth group over the previous year was happening all over America. There were hundreds of thousands with hearts ablaze for His presence and singing at the top of their lungs. The diverse crowd represented many colors, denominations, and ethnicities. Although our community had a measure of diversity, I had never experienced anything like that before! As a unified body, we had powerful times of repentance, weeping, and dynamic racial reconciliation, alongside times of explosive joy, hope, and celebration.

That afternoon, there was a surprise downpour. Hundreds of thousands of people were immediately soaked with the rain, but it seemed like no one left—we all continued to intercede for the nations. Up until that point, whenever I would begin to pray over the nations in a prayer meeting, my heart would swell and tears would begin to flow. But that day, my experience was exponentially greater. I lay prostrate on the muddy ground of the National Mall and I had a profound vision that would lay the foundation for the calling on my life.

In my vision, I saw the world being held in the palm of God's hand. I was amazed at how big God was and how small every other issue on the earth was in the palm of His hand. As I looked at the earth, I began to notice little fires breaking out all over the world. First it was just a few, and then it grew until there were hundreds and hundreds of fires. The fires were not large; they were all seemingly little flames on the little globe in God's hand. But then I noticed something else. The smoke from all of the flames began to rise up to the face of God. He breathed in the fragrance of the smoke and His heart was moved by their sacrifice of worship. In turn, He began to blow the wind of revival upon the earth. The revelation of Jesus and His salvation for mankind became brighter and clearer than ever before. Waves upon waves of people turned their hearts to Him and surrendered their lives. My vision encompassed an awakening of historic proportions, the likes of which I had never seen or read about before.

This vision consumed my life for the days, weeks, and months that followed. It established a trajectory for what I wanted to give my entire life to. And though I couldn't possibly understand it at the time, it also foreshadowed what would take place in many years to come.

CHAPTER 3

BRAZEN FAITH

Two years later, right after I graduated from high school, the first opportunity came to visit one of the nations listed on the sticky note in my room that had been there since I returned from my first mission trip years ago. My dad's coworker, a hero of mine in the missions world, was going to Afghanistan and had invited me along. The prayers that I had been praying for so many years were now starting to bear fruit! I also felt like the trip would be an opportunity for me to get out of the country and hear God's voice for the next season of my life.

I was stoked out of my mind for the opportunity. Some of my family and many of my friends, however, were unsettled. The terrorist attack on September 11, 2001, had rocked the world and our way of life had forever changed. Fear and paranoia toward the Middle East and Muslim culture were at an all time high across America. The US troops and allied forces had recently invaded Afghanistan. The world was in the middle of a full-blown war against terror.

This seemed to be all that the media was talking about and their narrative dominated the minds of most Americans. The more that people tried to convince me not to go, the more I felt to dig my heels into the Word of God over my life. I am sure most of the people cautioning me had good intentions, but I had been praying for so long for a door like this to open.

Ever since Brazil, I had a feeling that many voices would come with their opinions and thoughts, but there would be only One that mattered. I watched this happen with my parents when they made the risky choice to leave their hard-earned medical practice behind in Montana. I watched it happen with other bold leaders around me as they pursued God's call with reckless abandon. The resistance they attracted brought validation to the very voice they were following. They were unafraid. They were brazen. Yet this was my first experience in life where I was at a crossroads. I could either succumb to the fears of some of my friends and a few of my family members, appeasing their desire for my safety, or I could follow the voice of God into the dangerous unknown. The decision to go on this trip felt significant and it was: it would create a precedent of risk and faith in my life.

Along with the resistance among those around me, there were many other obstacles that stood against this trip becoming a reality. The Taliban had firm control of many of the cities in the nation. They had a history of abducting foreigners and holding them for ransom. They were merciless and brutal and used these situations to threaten, torture, and ultimately raise revenue from abductions to fund their war. The US State Department strongly warned Americans not to travel into Afghanistan along with a reminder that they would not be able to rescue any citizen who was abducted.

The last and most difficult obstacle was that the Afghan embassy in Washington, DC was not issuing visas to American citizens under any circumstances. Period.

When I explained all of these barriers to the wily and bright-eyed Indian missionary hero who invited me to go, he smiled at me and said, "But God will make a way, brother! Be bold and let's have an adventure together with God."

He had spent much of his ministry traveling in and out of Afghanistan and the surrounding Middle Eastern countries. He was currently pioneering a project to rebuild schools for girls that the Taliban had bombed. The Taliban's fundamentalist beliefs in radical Islam prohibited women from learning in school. This is a strong sentiment that still exists across many nations in the Middle East today.

After processing and praying with my parents, they officially gave me the green light to pursue the trip. I needed to raise $2,000 for plane tickets and expenses, as well as find a way to get the most elusive visa in the world. Both seemed impossible. I sent letters out to all my closest family and relatives and support began to roll in as people who believed in me backed this vision. I also sold some things that I owned and did anything and everything to scrape the money together. Making the trip possible became all-consuming. It was the only thing I cared about.

———

Upon the advice of my missionary friends, I went in person to the Afghan embassy in Washington, DC. I was told this was my best shot at getting a visa. Even so, the odds were slim to none. The ultimate goal, as I walked into the embassy that day, was to convince them to let an eighteen-year-old, blond-haired, blue-eyed American inside an active war zone so I could help rebuild schools for girls. Seemed like a real solid case to me!

During the three-and-a-half-hour drive up to the nation's capital, I prayed in the spirit and my confidence grew with every mile I drove. By the time I arrived, I was fully determined that there was no way I would be leaving that building until I had a visa stamped inside my passport. I would accept nothing less!

The man I talked to at the embassy was in total disbelief of my story. He could not fathom why I would want to go to his nation during so much turmoil and he kept discouraging me from trying to do it. He gave me several very compelling reasons not to go to his own country. I explained to him over and over again how this was a nation I had always wanted to visit. I shared that I was willing to give my life to help his people. He looked at me and said, "Well, are you truly willing to give your life right now? Because there is a high chance of that if you go."

Without skipping a beat, I responded, "Well, I guess I am willing to take my chances." I told him I was not going to leave until he gave me the visa. He smiled nervously and then stamped a ninety-day multiple-entry visa inside my passport. I could not hold in the rush of excitement! Expectation surged through my veins.

That moment, and the trip as a whole, created a framework in my life for chasing after God's heart for the nations. It also began a pattern of rushing into zones of conflict and persecution. My confidence grew as I refused to listen to the echos of other people's fear and anxiety. I had no idea at the time how much that foundation of risk, faith, and following the radical voice of God would impact my life in the years to come.

———

We spent the bulk of our time in isolated mountain villages. The people we encountered were peaceful, with warm and kind hearts. They received us with joy and would feed us their best goats, chickens, and fruit. I brought my guitar along on the trip and I would sit around the village well and play worship songs as people gathered around me. Very rarely could any of us understand each other—interpreters were limited. The people spoke in a tribal dialect of Farsi. They had also never met or heard a white American singing in English before.

Music, however, has a way of bringing people together and crossing the divide. Those times in the village with my guitar broke down all our walls and misconceptions about one another. I know I came in with so many wrong perceptions and stigmas about the culture, the people, and the religion. But singing each day with my guitar and a crowd of Afghanis changed everything for me. The power of music was bringing us together and God's presence showed up every single time.

We were advised by leaders inside the country to never stay the night in one of those villages. This was to avoid all chances of being abducted. We were encouraged to move into a better place of security or to just keep moving. But after spending all day building relationship, sharing stories, laughing, and eating together, it was so hard for us to leave. Many nights, we were invited to stay at the home of tribal leaders. We often stayed on the roof, as it was cooler than inside the house. We would fall asleep gazing at the clearest and brightest stars I had ever seen. It was magical.

It reminded me of the story of Abraham and the time God invited him outside his tent to "count the stars together." I always loved that story. Something about the audacity of God's playful request during Abraham's time of struggle enthralled me. Desperately clinging to the promise of becoming "the father of many nations" (Gen 17:5), Abraham was trapped inside a tent surrounded by nothing but his circumstances. All he could see was impossibility, hope deferred, and failure.

The reality of the situation is that the hopes of his lineage hung on the fact that his wife was barren and could not have any children. God wanted to remind Abraham of His promise again but did not want to do it while

Abraham was fixated on his problem. God wanted to give Abraham a change of scenery. So He invited him to count the stars.

Something about the stars pulls us into wonder and beauty, regardless of our circumstances. They remind us of how small we are and how big God is over everything. They also remind us that the human heart is hungry for beauty, wonder, and adventure. That is the life God is offering us. One that requires risk, courage, and faith to enter into its fullness.

While lying on the rooftop in Afghanistan that night and staring at the stars, I was pulled into a new realm of God's pleasure. I had persevered to follow His voice into the unknown, and though I didn't know it, He was guiding me into a life of brazen faith. A life that would continually pull me into the unexpected, and in some cases, defeat.

Of course, that night all I was aware of was the beauty of the stars and the pleasure of God's love.

CHAPTER 4

AUDIENCE OF ONE

Ever since my first trip to the Amazon at age twelve, I vowed that I was never going to college. My plan was very simple: finish high school and buy a one-way ticket to China or some other nation with hundreds of unreached people groups. I was content to live out my days wherever there was a need. I wanted to sow my entire life into the nations.

It wasn't that I felt I didn't have the brains for college. I did not have the same passion for school as my sisters, who pursued degrees at top schools and went on to become doctors and nurses. But I still graduated from high school with a 4.0 GPA. I was diligent in school and had a great work ethic. The reason college didn't appeal to me was simply that I carried an eagerness to *go* as soon as I could and not let anything hold me back.

My tune began to change, however, after I sent out my first few support letters for mission trips. The immense amount of work and time it took to raise money for just one trip was far beyond what I imagined. My dream was to be living in the nations and doing trips full-time! I began to realize the current model of support letters was not sustainable long term. My dad was also in charge of over thirty full-time missionaries for his new job as the missions pastor at our thriving church. The number one issue the missionaries faced was lack of funding. I hated the thought of always asking for money or spending half of my year fundraising in America while the nations waited. I wanted to be full-time overseas.

This and several other factors pushed me toward looking into college options with my dad. We took a trip together to visit four campuses across the country. They were all in different states and carried completely different ambiences. The last campus we visited, however, was an experience unlike the rest. Our plane arrived late because of a bad spring storm that rolled into Oklahoma with hail and sporadic tornados. There was a monsoon of rain and wind, which caused us to be late for the weekly chapel service, our first stop on campus. My dad went to look for parking as I ran up the hill into the golden-colored '70s looking auditorium. The campus was very dated and looked like something straight out of the Jetsons cartoons.

As I opened the massive wooden double doors to the chapel, I was completely drenched from my run up the hill. But none of that even mattered as soon as I heard the crowd of thousands of students singing at the top of their lungs with their hands lifted high in the air. It seemed like everyone was worshiping their hearts out as the chaplain of the university prayed for the filling of the Holy Spirit in a fresh way. I knew at that very moment that the rest of the visit to Oral Roberts University was irrelevant. That was exactly where I was supposed to be. The atmosphere was filled with God's presence. It was stunning and felt just like home.

———

I had the perfect vision in my mind for how my first year of college would look. I was coming out of my high school years riding high. I had worked hard to become the main worship leader at our youth group. I was finally excelling at music and songwriting, and our band was sounding really good. I was hosting large worship events in the region where hundreds would gather. We even captured a few of them on live albums that were now spreading around the world. On top of that, my football team won the state championship for the first time in history and that success was widely known across the region. I was dating the most amazing, gorgeous, God-fearing girl I had ever met. Kate was going into her senior year of high school and while I knew moving to Tulsa would be a challenge for our relationship, I had this deep knowing that we were going to end up together. All cylinders were firing and there was only one way to go from here: higher, better, and farther.

I was right on course for my life to get launched like never before. Even though I was not initially thrilled about living in Oklahoma, I knew that many notable worship leaders, evangelists, missionaries, and pastors were catapulted into ministry from Oral Roberts University. And I believed that I was next in line. It was my turn. Just as I had seen older friends get launched into their callings and destinies from TheCall gathering in Washington, DC a few years earlier, I knew college was now my moment, and I was ready.

Of course, none of that even came close to happening that first year on campus. In fact, it was pretty much the exact opposite. I tried to get plugged into worship and missions, but nothing seemed to work out. My roommate that year wasn't even a believer. He would purposefully blast explicit rap music at insane volumes all day long to drown out any worship music I would play. I failed miserably at every band and worship tryout at the university and the surrounding churches. I began to second-guess every vision, dream, and word from God that I had ever received. I was devastated. It felt like a failure to launch. My ego was annihilated.

I was also carrying disappointment from three of the most respected spiritual leaders in my life during high school. Within the course of a few months, they had all independently been caught in affairs and left their wives and kids behind because of it. Some of them had even left the faith entirely. It was a crushing blow to me as they were leaders I really looked up to in so many ways.

At one point, I just stopped playing my guitar. I hid it under my dorm room bed and diverted my focus to studying business. I even thought about ditching college once and for all after just one semester. My heart grew cold and disillusioned. I did not run up to the front anymore when worship began at chapel. The fire felt like it was starting to die.

Then, one night in my dorm room, God deeply encountered me. All my friends were headed out to the local dollar theater for the 11:00 p.m. showing of whatever random movie they had playing. This was a tradition that we did every weekend as a dorm. For some reason, I stayed back. Probably just to feel sorry for myself. But there in the midst of my brokenness and shattered expectations, I heard the Holy Spirit speak.

"Pick up your guitar and find me in the stairwell." For a moment, I thought maybe I was having a mental breakdown. *Was that God or my own mind?* But then the voice came again and louder this time. "Pick up your guitar and find me in the stairwell."

I lived on the eighth floor of a dormitory tower with only one elevator and a long stairwell next to it. It was an old building and often the elevator would get stuck, forcing us to climb eight flights of stairs a few times per week, at least. It was not a pleasant stairwell. It was made of cold concrete and steel handrails, like the stairwells you might find in a typical parking garage. It did, however, have very pretty acoustics.

For the first time in many months, I picked up my guitar. It was out of tune and so dirty that I had to dust it off with an old T-shirt. Nothing in me really wanted to strum a single chord, but I was curious to see if I was really hearing God or just my own weird thoughts. After a thorough tuning, I took the guitar to the stairwell and began to play a few chords in that cold, quiet, echoey space. The frequencies rang out against the walls and almost anything I played or sang sounded pretty epic. It felt so good to hold and play my guitar again.

In that moment, apart from the great acoustics, something real happened inside me when I opened my mouth to sing. A fountain of words, tears, and life poured out of me. The well of my heart and emotions that had been dammed up with pain, confusion, and disappointment began to open. My first few strums and songs were not pretty, by any means. But they were authentic. I began to feel the nearness of God again for the first time in a while. Before long, I was a weeping, snotty, singing mess. While I did not know it at the time, God was removing a spirit of performance and man-pleasing from me. He was inviting me into a realm of being known by Him, and killing the desire to be known by people. He was showing me how to play for an audience of One.

The stairwell became a hideout, my secret place. It was my own personal Cave of Addulam. In the hiddenness, God was there. I began to get my song back. The most raw, honest, and passionate sounds, melodies, and lyrics poured from my heart. What began as weekly times with God turned into daily moments, and then multiple times per day. My heart was coming fully alive again.

———

Oral Roberts was a campus full of musicians, many of whom were touring with big contemporary Christian music bands or already serving full-time gigs in their local megachurches. Some had been chewed up and spat out by the industry or the church. They just needed a fresh baptism of fire. As I met friends who were burned out, over church, or just needing a fresh encounter with God, I would invite them into my times of worship. I shared the things that were happening in my heart and encouraged them to come join me.

One by one, they would stream into my dorm room on Friday nights. There was no agenda, no performance, and no crowd. We had beautiful, unplanned, and spontaneous times of worship together. It was our hearts laid bare before the Lord, exposing our need for more of Him.

There were nights we got so lost in worship together that we even forgot what time it was. We saw the sunrise out of my little dorm room window and were floored that we had worshiped through the night. God was up to something and the word was spreading across campus about what was happening on the eighth floor of Wesley Dorm.

It wasn't long before my dorm room became so cramped and stuffy that it was clear we were running out of room. I had the idea to move the worship nights to my friend's coffee shop across the street. I knew it would change the dynamic and expose the hiddenness of what was happening. But then again, I thought, maybe it was time to take our private prayer meeting public. I was also in a men's only dormitory, so girls could never join in. You could say that the move would officially make it an equal opportunity ministry!

My friend offered us a room connected to his coffee shop and was even willing to stay open for us so we could worship through the night. We planned an all-night worship event and spread the details by word of mouth. We didn't have a name, logo, or even proper language for what we were doing. But that didn't seem to matter.

The vision spread like wildfire and people continued to stream in during the first set on a Friday night. The coffee shop was slammed and almost everyone there was a college student. It was mind blowing. There were so many other things to do on a college campus on Friday night. Besides that, the other college ministries in town were actually way more attractive than what we were doing. Tulsa has some of the most well-funded churches in America, and they had tons of very organized and well-marketed events. Our worship night was anything but that. It was very raw, unpolished, and pretty messy. But people came anyway.

My friends and I immediately started planning for a twenty-four-hour gathering the very next month. As we made plans, we also started brainstorming names. What should we call this thing God was doing? None of us were into building a brand or even a ministry. "Tulsarusalem," as many still call Tulsa, had plenty of churches, ministries, and events. It didn't need one more. We knew, however, that we needed a name, at the very least.

We kicked around few ideas until we landed on the story of the men on the road to Emmaus in Luke 24. It takes place right after the manifestation of the greatest miracle in the history of mankind: Christ's resurrection. As two of His disciples are traveling, Jesus encounters them on the road. This story seemed to resonate with every single one of us.

> Now that same day two of them were going to a village called Emmaus, about seven miles from Jerusalem.
>
> They were talking with each other about everything that had happened. As they talked and discussed these things with each other, Jesus himself came up and walked along with them; but they were kept from recognizing him.
>
> He asked them, "What are you discussing together as you walk along?"
>
> They stood still, their faces downcast. One of them, named Cleopas, asked him, "Are you the only one visiting

Jerusalem who does not know the things that have happened there in these days?"

"What things?" he asked.

Luke 24:13-19

What we connected with, initially, was that the disciples or friends of Jesus were completely unaware of the season they were living in. They were so blinded by their own disappointment that they couldn't see that everything had changed. They had lost all hope and trust in the promises of God. As they lamented Jesus' unfulfilled promises, they had no idea that they stood face to face with the *risen Christ.*

This story felt identical to the season I was in. I was carrying so many amazing promises from God when I left high school—the youth group in revival, the gathering at the National Mall, Afghanistan, and all the momentum I had experienced and prophetic words I had received. I felt like everything would come to fruition when I stepped on the campus and I would be catapulted to the next level of global ministry for the entire world to see! HA!

When absolutely none of that happened, I became discouraged, hopeless, and disillusioned. I actually purposefully forgot some of God's promises over my life and tried my best to move on. God crashed into the stairwell, however, and everything changed. In what felt like my darkest hour of bewilderment, He appeared and reminded me that He had been there all along. I was unaware that He was still moving, still working, and knew every desire of my heart.

In Luke 24, Jesus began to teach the two disciples and remind them what the scriptures said about Him. He tested their hunger as they approached the village by continuing "on as if he were going farther" (Luke 24:28). There goes our sneaky Jesus! We do not always talk about this in sermons, systematic theology, or Bible classes, but there was definitely a wily side to God walking in the flesh! He loved to mess with people and keep them on their toes. It always worked. The disciples walking to Emmaus invited Him for dinner and their eyes were opened as they broke bread and ate together.

This was a powerful moment. Intimate fellowship—such as the breaking of bread—is the context in which our eyes become aware of who God really is. This was true for me. It was why the stairwell sessions were so necessary to formulate a real and raw relationship with the divine Creator of the universe. The spirit of performance was scourged from my heart. All that I truly desired was His presence.

As my friends and I sat huddled together reading Luke 24 in the coffee shop the week after that first gathering, we came to a line that made us all stop right in the middle of reading.

> When he was at the table with them, he took bread, gave thanks, broke it and began to give it to them. Then their eyes were opened and they recognized him, and he disappeared from their sight. They asked each other, "Were not our hearts burning within us while he talked with us on the road and opened the Scriptures to us?"
>
> Luke 24:30-32

Our hearts *were* burning within us! That was it! That one line gave us language for what we were experiencing! It was the only way to describe what was truly taking place. While we did not have theology or framework at the time for an expression of day and night worship, we did all feel that His presence made us come alive! That was all we lived for. It burned the disappointment, compromise, and lethargy off of our lives. No formula, agenda, slick ministry program, or production could do that. It was just the raw Presence and weight of His glory that kept us fighting sleep all night and pressing in for more!

We all agreed that this was it, and so we called this thing—this moment, this momentum, this movement—The Burn.

We knew it would probably get misinterpreted, that it may sound cultish, or confuse some people, but we really didn't care. We didn't want to do this for acceptance, popularity, or fame. We wanted to do this for Him and Him alone.

That day we left our brainstorming session with the name "Burn," and I never looked back.

CHAPTER 5

A SPIRIT OF RELIGION

Over the next three years, I felt the wind of God blowing on my life, and the path forward became clearer and clearer to me. The Burn started to grow and expand across the entire city. We gathered almost twice per month for twelve to twenty-four hours of nonstop worship and prayer. There was a waiting list of worship leaders and musicians eager to join the next Burn. The most sought-after two-hour sets were between midnight and 6:00 a.m. It was during those night watches that we experienced profound moves of God.

Worship leaders and pastors who were constantly pouring into their own churches would show up in the middle of the night to get a fresh touch from God. Even when there were hardly any people in the room,

God was present. It was raw, passionate, and powerful. Worship teams came prepared with their set lists of forty songs only to find that midway through the third song, the Holy Spirit would show up and take over their hearts, souls, and sound! There was a transcendent peace that broke the back of striving and the heavy performance-based religious spirit in the town. It often seemed like God waited to do His best and deepest work when there were fewer people present.

God would touch, heal, and deliver anyone who could stay and wait on Him. Reconciliation took place between family members and leaders in ministry who held grudges against each other for years. A lady was healed of a cancerous tumor when she fell asleep in worship. She woke up to discover her tumor was completely gone!

These testimonies became a weekly occurrence. We decided to put out a testimony box so people could share the stories, testimonies, visions, and words God gave them during worship. I read every single one of them.

Hearts were lit on fire in God's presence. We gained a positive reputation in town with some of the bigger and more well-known ministries. We purposely maintained a neutral position and chose not to affiliate with one single church. This enabled us to bless the city and not create competition. Although, some ministries still chose to view us that way.

———

I was still finishing my business degree when I decided to record my first album. It was a dream of mine to capture some of the "stairwell songs." One of my good friends was doing an internship at the university recording studio, so we snuck into the studio after class hours and began laying down some of the songs. My friend was an incredible musician and he also knew all the best musicians on campus. So many people came alongside me to donate their time, energy, and talents to make it a reality. I had always dreamed of capturing my own album of original songs—and this would be just the first of many. We celebrated the album release as I kicked off the first two hours of a 24-hour Burn playing every song on the album. That night felt like a convergence moment for me.

Around the same time, I was offered a job as a part-time worship leader at a local church. I had been attending there for a few months and really loved how they pressed into the things of the spirit. They worshiped with abandon and I experienced a freedom to explore spiritual spaces that many other churches did not leave room for. I was drawn to that freedom and excited to be more involved.

The job stretched me as a musician and a leader more than I could have ever imagined. I was responsible, along with another leader, for a Tuesday night healing service, Wednesday night intercession service, Thursday night band rehearsal, and Sunday morning and Sunday night services. Not only that, but the church also hosted at least one weekend conference per month. That meant one out of every four weekends included an additional Friday night, Saturday morning, and Saturday night service. It was a lot of work for a part-time position! But I was grateful for the opportunity to grow, try out my own songs, and meet amazing speakers, leaders, and heroes—many of whom are still my friends to this day.

God was also showing up in profound ways and I witnessed healings, miracles, salvations, and the power of God manifest before my eyes more than I ever had before. Through it all, however, there was an underlying dimension of control that I couldn't quite understand. I felt it, but I couldn't identify it.

———

While I was finishing my business degree, continuing to lead The Burn, and working my new job as a worship leader, Kate was 10,000 miles away on a very isolated island in the middle of the South Pacific. She was on the outreach portion of a six-month missions school and had absolutely zero contact with the outside world.

Over the previous five years of high school and then college, I had never once talked to her about marriage. I did not want to be a couple that made promises we could not keep. The romantic in me also wanted to completely surprise her with the ring and not plan our engagement like it seemed so many others were doing.

When she was on her outreach near Fiji, I had an encounter with the Lord where I knew it was time to buy a ring and make a move! I saved up all the money I could and custom designed a ring that I thought she would love. Although she had no idea about any of this, the moment she returned, I was convinced that she would be ready to give her all to the nations and become the most perfect companion to follow God's plan for our lives.

Her outreach, however, was a total disaster. There was considerable drama with her school leaders as well as a lack of purpose: they were living with a mostly Christian tribe on a far-flung, isolated island. To top it off, she got stung by one of the most poisonous jelly fish in the Pacific Ocean. She laid almost completely paralyzed for an entire day and was told by the tribal leaders the poison from the jelly fish may reach her heart and she would die.

She returned from that experience and told me she was *never* going to do missions ever again. She also never wanted to travel again. In her mind, that experience completely ruined any future in missions. I was completely demoralized. Traveling, ministry, and missions were all I ever wanted to do. Kate knew that, so the fact that she said all this to me was further proof of how traumatic her experience was. She was completely done and over it.

This presented me with some of the biggest questions of my adult life. Kate and I had pretty much grown up together since we started dating when we were sixteen and seventeen years old. I knew from the moment I laid eyes on her at church that we were going to be together one day. She was the only real girlfriend I had ever had in my life. We had fought for connection and navigated the years of distance while I was away in college and she stayed back home in Virginia. And now I finally had the green light from the Lord to go for it. Except, she didn't want anything to do with missions.

Yet, I kept coming back to the same truth. I was so in love with her that I could not let her go. And I believed God would somehow change her heart in all of this. I did not know how, but I was convinced it would happen. I made a total and complete surprise proposal in the spring of 2005 and she said yes!

———

We set a wedding date for December of that same year. A few months after our engagement, Kate flew to Oklahoma for a few months to find a job and spend time preparing for our life together. At the request of the church where I was on staff, we agreed to do our marriage counseling with one of their associate pastors. That ended up being one the biggest mistakes we could ever make.

That first day we arrived at his office to share our history—how we fell in love and where we felt God leading us. Kate was still getting over her recent horrible missions experience. I was confident that this church and this pastor could help guide us into healing and wholeness and prepare us for an amazing marriage together. We were bubbling with excitement and eager to grow.

Instead of talking, however, the first thing he had us do was take a personality test. It was the kind where you fill in the bubbles with pencil marks and they review it and let us know how we did. That took about fifteen minutes to complete. Afterward, the pastor looked at us and said there was not much more to talk about until he saw the results, and to come back next week for the next session.

The next week we walked into his office with the same giddiness and excitement as the week before. We were curious to see the results of our personality test and hopeful that we would get to share a little bit of our story as well. As we sat down, the pastor looked at us with the most solemn expression and said, "You are not going to get married. I will not allow it. After seeing your test results, I cannot give my stamp of approval on this marriage in any way."

We both stared at him for what felt like an eternity. Finally, I smiled, because I thought it was surely some kind of joke. It was a little twisted and crooked but I knew he *couldn't* be serious.

Oh, he surely was. "Kate's test showed that she is completely fragile and cowers," he went on to say. "Sean, your test shows that you are overbearing and controlling. My best guess is that you will be exhibiting physical abuse on her in less than ten years." Then he looked directly at Kate and said, "Do not marry him."

We were absolutely stunned. I couldn't believe that a member of our own staff would come up with something so crazy. He did not even know us. He did not ask us questions or hear our story. Instead, he cast a massive judgment over our marriage and our future. Before we left his office, he told us that he alerted the entire church staff to the test results. He also noted that they were all concerned.

At that point, my anger began to openly manifest. I am not a typically angry person except when my "justice switch" gets flipped. It flipped really hard and really quickly in that moment. "You did WHAT?!" I shouted. "Not only is that completely illegal for a counselor to do, but why didn't you come to us first with your concerns? Why go and gossip to the entire church about test results we got by FILLING IN THE BUBBLES ON A PAPER?!" I stormed out of that meeting.

———

Everything changed at the church from that point on. Rumors started to circulate about our relationship—not a single one was true. The atmosphere was toxic with religious manipulation. It was the first time I had ever felt that. I grew up learning to honor authority, even when I did not agree. But this was something different.

That pastor continued to call Kate, begging her not to marry me, all the way up until the day of our wedding! Not only did the pastors, leaders, and staff treat us differently, but a dark cloud hung over everything we did there. The excitement and zeal for helping create a worship department that was vibrant, prophetic, and cutting edge disappeared. Not only that, but Kate did not want to step foot back into that church as long as she lived. The season and time there ended abruptly when we chose to walk away.

What was supposed to be a blissful time of engagement turned into instant drama, tragedy, and pain for me and Kate. She was already completely cold to the idea of travel and missions. Now we could add ministry to that list as well. How were we supposed to get married when the only two things I ever wanted to do in life were completely out of the question?

My heart sank with discouragement as I struggled to understand the promises we once received. Even the momentum I'd gained from the past three years running The Burn felt like it was sucked out of me.

Once again, everything in my life felt contradictory to the path I anticipated. What began as a season of momentum and growth felt like it was crashing down around us.

CHAPTER 6

THE HOLY HARASSER

Despite all the disappointments we were facing together, I was still madly in love with my fiancée. She was the most beautiful person, inside and out, I had ever met. Regardless of any test results, pastor, or the opinions of an entire church, we knew we were called to be together.

I had to push aside my expectations for that season and let God heal both of us in the months leading up to our wedding day. We had the fear of missions and the fear of ministry to overcome, but I refused to lose hope. Kate and I believed our connection and commitment to each other were stronger than any of those fears. While we walked through this process of healing, I decided to refocus my energy from leading worship and dove headfirst into business.

I grew up watching and listening to global missionaries. Much like my parents, most of them sacrificed their entire careers in order to pour themselves out like an offering on the nations and the people groups God called them to. The one issue that always seemed to be the highest source of struggle and anxiety among them, however, was money.

I witnessed so many incredible people who were unable to fully walk out their callings and dreams in the nations because they did not have the resources to see it happen. They were dependent on donors, fundraisers, and trips back to the West to generate the funds necessary to continue. I always felt so bad for them. Money was, and is, a constant struggle. They were at the mercy of the generosity of others to accomplish what was right in front of them. I saw it as a huge distraction. Oftentimes, the more charismatic the personality, and the better they could communicate publicly, the more funds they earned to sustain them. That meant raising funds was even more difficult for the missionaries who were more introverted.

I knew there was a better way. I did not want to follow that model and be held captive or mandated to leave the very place I was called to in order to raise funds. In my mind, the answer was simple: make a ton of money. *What if I throw myself into business and build something that can sustain my family long-term overseas?* I thought. I figured that if I put in the time now, then I could launch my mission work later and not have a care in the world. I would be able to go wherever I wanted and do whatever I wanted. For me, that idea represented ultimate freedom from the current system.

As I was finishing my last semester of college, the solution came in the form of a business, and I started a real estate company with two good friends of mine. One of the guys was a recent college graduate and the other was a wealthy businessman in town that took me under his wing. He helped fund our new real estate venture.

I had worked really hard to graduate toward the top of my class. I had incredible professors, many of whom were independently wealthy and only taught because they wanted to invest in the next generation. Often, our economics class would open with bold prayers and declarations for God to impart strategies to generate kingdom wealth. I really felt like real estate was that strategy, and so we built Three Musketeers Properties. We had business cards printed and a logo created. This was my season to make a ton of money that would lead to funding my own ministry!

It was 2005 and the housing market was pretty hot. We were buying and flipping homes like crazy. We would spend hours researching bank foreclosure lists, estate sales, county tax sales and go anywhere and everywhere we could find cheap homes that needed work. We would then turn them around in a two to three-month window and sell them for a decent profit. We went to business lunches with brokers, real estate gurus, and anyone we thought could help us. We were young, driven, and really presumptuous. We would often drive hundreds of miles per week across Oklahoma and Texas looking for the cheapest properties to buy and flip. Business was good.

Just before Kate and I got married, I even purchased my first house—a little three bedroom, two bathroom brick home with a fenced-in backyard. It was the perfect starter home for a new family. I was excited to be making money, providing for my future and family, and I was even more excited to show our new home to my wife.

———

Kate and I were married in our hometown of Virginia Beach that fall and we had the most joyful wedding. Since both of our parents were pastors and we had so many friends in town, we invited 700 people! We did not have a large budget to work with—I was just launching our business and Kate was working as a waitress and saving every penny she could for our honeymoon. It was definitely a low-budget affair, but we did not care. I don't think many others cared, either. We bought a giant fondu fountain and had desserts, fruit, and cheese you could pluck with a toothpick and run under the endless flow of dark chocolate. It felt like a dream and I wouldn't change anything about it. We worshiped. We partied. We danced. Our friends, parents, and leaders prayed and prophesied over us. It was perfect.

Part of our wedding gift from my parents was airline miles to use for our honeymoon. My dad had saved a bunch of miles from all of his mission trips and we gladly accepted! Because of the nature of using airline miles, there was only one city that worked for our dates and did not have black-outs. Shortly after the wedding reception, Kate and I were on our way to Venice, Italy!

We purposely did not plan where we would go or stay during our time in Venice. That was kind of my style (and in many ways, it still is). I wanted to go on an adventure with my wife and let the wind blow us wherever it may. Although Kate was a little apprehensive about traveling abroad after her last mission experience, she allowed the gleeful high of our long-awaited honeymoon together to override the apprehension. I am sure glad that she did! We ended up renting the tiniest car I had ever seen and traveling through Italy, Slovenia, Austria, Germany, and France. We stayed at the cheapest accommodations we could find and ate anywhere that looked good (and affordable). It was magical, fun, invigorating and was our first international trip together.

When we returned to Tulsa, I threw myself into the real estate company while Kate worked at an optometrist office and took classes at the local community college. I was still leading and giving vision to the monthly Burn gatherings during this time, as well. A friend of mine oversaw the administration and planning of it all so I could give more time to my real estate company. After our traumatic church experience, I was not eager to jump back into any sort of ministry. In my compartmentalized view of life, I kept the "ministry box" at a safe distance while not disturbing everything else.

Kate and I settled into our new home and began building a life togeth-er—a normal and safe suburban American life. We had two dogs, a little Mitsubishi convertible, and we went to the movies on the weekend. It felt really good—for a season.

It did not take long, however, before this normal life also started to feel uncomfortable in the deepest layers of my heart.

———

Sometimes it is the most unexpected things that knock us out of our comfort zones. On November 12, 2006, I woke up to the most tragic news. I will never forget that moment because it marked our lives forever.

Our community in Tulsa had become the family of believers partici-pating in The Burn: a chorus of young worshipers, intercessors, musicians, and burning hearts doing life together in the Presence of God. These were the people we were investing our lives into. It was organic, raw, and felt like the closest thing I had ever experienced to the book of Acts.

One of the worshipers—Bethany Swift—was part of this close-knit community. She had recently gone away to college a few hours from Tulsa but would come back often to lead worship at The Burn. She always chose the sessions in the middle of the night when no one was there. She embod-ied a new generation of worshiper that was sold out for the Presence of God above the praise of men. She had the purest heart and most precious song before the Lord.

That morning, I received the news that she had died in a head-on colli-sion as she was driving back to her dorm room in Shawnee, Oklahoma. This sent shockwaves through our community and the entire region. Everyone knew Bethany, and everyone loved her.

Kate was so overcome with grief that she could not even stand up in our room that morning. She wept uncontrollably for our friend. She stayed that way for at least three days, barely even leaving our house.

After giving Kate what little comfort I could, I drove to Bethany's parents' house. There was a line of cars in their driveway and a crowd gathered inside the house. Just hours after hearing the news of their daughter's passing, her parents were seated at her piano, singing their hearts out to Jesus. It was both gut-wrenching and absolutely holy.

There was weeping and pain. There was deep sorrow and anguish. But there was an atmosphere of worship unlike any I encountered before. It was the first time I witnessed Psalm 34:18 lived out: "The Lord is close to the brokenhearted."

Bethany's parents handed me a guitar when I got there and asked me to sing a song. I could barely stand up and wept my way through a few chords before I collapsed to the ground. Her father, who had just lost his beautiful eighteen-year-old daughter, wrapped his arms around me to comfort me.

I remember thinking, *How in the world can he be doing this right now? What kind of anchor of hope does he possess that I do not? What kind of surrender is in his heart that I don't have?* Those questions sat in the depths of my heart. I stayed for hours and hours and just worshiped. It was all that we could do. No one had answers. No one understood what happened or why. Our only response was to thank God for her life and beg for His mercy over ours.

———

Driving home that evening, I experienced a shift in my heart. All my pain and disappointment from the previous season had vanished. I was undone with a fresh baptism of love and a renewed passion to give my all to God. It was sobering. It was raw. I was wrecked.

I walked into our perfect home, with our two dogs, our convertible, and our nice little life. Kate's eyes were swollen from weeping. I looked her straight in the eyes and told her that everything was about to change. We are only given one chance to live, I said, and we are not going to waste it in pursuit of the American dream. We had to give it all to God.

The Holy Spirit came in the following days of mourning and began to speak to me. I experienced something beyond comfort and peace. In fact, many times it felt like the exact opposite. I know that bringing us comfort is one of His main job descriptions. Kate and I both felt that aspect of His nature as we mourned, and we needed that grace on our lives. But I also encountered a different side of His personality.

God exposed every area of self-sufficiency and self-reliance in my life. He shattered the fears, pain, and disappointment that held me back. He became what I call the "Holy Harasser" in my life.

I knew that the trajectory I was establishing for my life was one built out of caution and in reaction to the hurt from past ministry endeavors. Kate was also carrying the weight of her first missions experience and the burden of hurt from the church. Yet, all of that seemed to dissolve away as we were confronted with the sobering reality of how short our lives really are. We are never promised tomorrow.

Kate and I realized that it was time to make today count. We were responsible for this moment, and for our lives. Bethany's extravagant life of worship, and her sudden departure into eternity, made us come to grips with our own existence. We began asking questions about what we were truly living for. The Holy Spirit was harassing us—challenging us—to take the next steps into fulfilling our mandate on this earth.

———

I met with my business partners and explained what the Lord was showing me and that it was time for us to leave Tulsa. I felt bad, in many ways, because we had worked so hard and things were just starting to move forward for us. We were gaining traction and making good profit on the homes we sold.

In fact, we had spent the last month working on a massive thirty-five home acquisition across North Texas. We were going to buy them as fore-closures for fifty cents on the dollar and planned to flip them and sell to investors out of Arizona. It was a bonafide win that would net our new company millions of dollars.

But my heart was being drawn in a different direction. The moment I had been building since college was now here. I knew it was now or never.

The Holy Harasser continued to fill my dreams each night with the echo of Psalm 132, a passage that also ministered to me deeply during the stairwell season.

> He swore an oath to the Lord,
> he made a vow to the Mighty One of Jacob:
> "I will not enter my house
> or go to my bed,
> I will allow no sleep to my eyes
> or slumber to my eyelids,
> till I find a place for the Lord,
> a dwelling for the Mighty One of Jacob."
>
> Psalm 132:3-5

In college, this verse drove me to pick up my guitar again for the audience of One. It awakened the song that I once thought was dead inside of me. I had once again reached a moment in life where there was no turning back, and this verse filled my heart and mind.

I honestly did not know where we would go. I did not even have the answers for why we were leaving. I just knew we were called to something more than the life we were living. Our lives were meant to be poured out in worship to God and laid down in love for the nations. The best place to start seemed like right here in our own nation. We didn't know what it would look like. I had my guitars, we had a passion for authentic worship and prayer, and we had each other. Heading out on the road to spread the heart of worship felt like our only option if we were going to truly live.

Within a few weeks of Bethany's passing, we sold almost everything we owned. I put our house on the market, we sold our convertible, and we even said goodbye to one of our dogs. We packed up everything else we owned and put it in storage. It was a foolish decision. It was reckless. It was answering a call to the brazen lifestyle.

Kate and I packed up our 1998 black Toyota Camry with everything we thought we would need to live. It was weighed down with sleeping bags, pillows, guitars, my loud and obnoxious beagle puppy, a few sets of clothes, and revival history books. We pulled out from our driveway with the back bumper of the car scraping the ground.

Kate looked in my eyes with tears rolling down her cheeks and said, "Where are we going, Sean?"

"I don't really know," I said. "But we are on a journey pursuing His presence and we're going to give our entire lives to this."

CHAPTER 7

THE BURN

It turns out that my idea to live out of our car was not quite as romantic or charming as I thought it would be. The grandiose ideas in my mind about this holy pursuit of God were not taking shape as I had hoped. I kept waiting for God to come through and validate our crazy decision to those who were watching this unfold. I hoped it would begin with my own parents.

They were beginning to have some concerns, as any good parents would, while watching their child jump into the unknown. We left behind everything I had built, all of the preparations I had made for a safe and financially stable life together. There was no turning back now.

My parents had seen how hard I worked in college to earn my degree and finish at the top of my class. They knew about the real estate venture that was catching momentum and growing exponentially. They understood my desire to want to create stability, peace, and a home for our new marriage to thrive as we planned for a family. Then they watched me abruptly snap and decide to give that all away. When my dad called with some genuine concerns, I had to remind him that much of this was actually his fault.

They had modeled a life of extravagant sacrifice for the gospel. They carried the willingness to lay it all down the moment the wind of the Spirit blew them in a different direction. When we moved from the brilliant and financially viable Montana practice that my dad spent over a decade building, I took note. My ten-year-old eyes were wide open and aware. I recognized—while hating it and pushing against it at the time—the cost they were willing to pay to leave it all and follow the voice of God. They weighed the impact it would have on their four children and the life of predictability we had grown accustomed to. In a moment's notice, they just left it all. Journeying into the unknown on the East Coast, we all thought it was so crazy. Until it wasn't.

I reminded him that when we moved, our family thrived in our new environment. My sisters and I were afforded many opportunities we didn't have in our little mountain town. We all had significant encounters with God and were stretched in our understanding of the world. We saw and experienced different cultures, perspectives, and mindsets. My parents had made a brilliant decision and "wisdom was proved right by her actions" (Luke 7:35).

———

The problem for me and Kate, however, was that we didn't know exactly what was next. I had always been a diligent planner. I loved knowing the greater purpose of a decision and defining the steps that would help us reach our end goal. After leaving Tulsa, I faced inner turmoil and frustration because I did not have any answers.

Our pursuit of God's presence was authentic, but the outcome felt really vague. We simply packed up our car and drove away, asking God where we should go and who we should serve. Many friends, leaders, and mentors tried to help guide us as we embarked on our new adventure. Their voices didn't always agree on where we should go and what we should do. Although we were not launched or covered by a particular church or ministry, we felt covered by many advisors, friends, and ultimately the Holy Spirit.

I knew God was up to something when complete strangers would reach out to us and invite us to come to their city to host evenings of prayer and worship. We felt a green light from God to respond to almost any and all requests with an emphatic YES, without imposing conditions. In other words, we weren't asking for any money.

Kate and I spent many days traveling from city to city, community to community, sharing our hearts through worship, prayer, and exhortation when I didn't know where we were going to sleep that night. I didn't even know how we would pay for the tank of gas to get to the next town. We felt directionless, and at times, I felt entirely helpless.

That was a new space for me. I was more dependent on God's voice every day than any other time in my life. I also carried the weight and anxiety of having my beautiful and innocent bride on this journey. My desire to provide for her and "prove" myself as a good husband was at an all-time high. Some days I felt sick to my stomach at the thought that I might be leading her down a road with a dead end.

Little did I know that God was fashioning a grassroots network of relationship largely created from my high school friends, college buddies, and through so many who had heard about The Burn. What began as an unknown adventure started to form into a type of itinerate worship ministry. We were taking The Burn on the road.

———

We accepted invitations to some of the most random places imaginable. Requests would roll in from "a friend of a friend who knew someone at church" who wanted us to come to their gathering. It was random and completely unpredictable. During those days, we didn't have social media (besides our static Myspace page) to help us spread the word. We couldn't boost posts on Facebook to spread the news or provide booking forms for people to fill out. Everything happened by word of mouth.

Somehow, despite our limitations, what we were doing seemed to go viral. Many believers were curious about this "burn thing" that started in Tulsa, Oklahoma. They could not fathom why college students would choose to stay up all night long just to worship Jesus. It seemed so counter-cultural and crazy. We became a gathering mechanism for the hungry, the skeptics, the cynics, and the rejects who felt like they just did not fit into the current church and worship paradigms.

At the same time, several legitimate and inviting job opportunities came my way from thriving churches across the country. All of the locations were great, the jobs were consistent, and the money offered was good, but I felt like I would be selling out by accepting any of them. I wanted nothing less than God's best.

Now that we were taking The Burn beyond Tulsa, I still believed it needed to stay neutral in order to rally and unify the Church. God was calling us to create a new wine skin to hold the new wine He was pouring out. Our heart was to bring churches from different backgrounds, ethnicities, and denominations together to worship under one manner and unto one Man. We knew in our hearts that the new wine was not in one church or one denomination—it is found in the entire cluster, the body of Christ. We continued to travel wherever God would open doors with the purpose of planting Burn worship and prayer "furnaces" in every city and community we visited. All of these communities just needed a little spark to ignite a fire that would continue to burn well beyond our short visit.

We filled the most unsuspecting and unassuming places with the sound of worship. We were not exclusive and went to as many places as possible to stoke the fires of worship and prayer. One night, it was a little baptist church in Fort Smith, Arkansas, that was definitely not Spirit filled. The next night, we worshiped at a workout gym in Tyler, Texas, where we rolled out the barbells and elliptical machines to make room for the band. Then it was a living room in someone's house in Bartlesville, Oklahoma, an outdoor patio in Shreveport, Louisiana, and so on. If people were ready to unite and worship Jesus together within a 500-mile radius of where we were driving, we were there!

At every single gathering we experienced a profound sense of expectation. Just as it had happened in Tulsa, where it all began, every night we were filled with a sense of awe and wonder, humbled by God's presence. We worshiped our hearts out and then, at some point in the night, I would explain the vision for The Burn. Then we would worship and pray some more, and leaders in the room would commit to carrying the torch of this fire forward. It was in those moments that we knew that was exactly what we were called to do. It was in those moments that our leap of faith made perfect sense.

Then there were times when it was so awkward that it felt like pulling teeth to get anyone to sing, pray, and engage. We left those nights confused, perplexed, and scratching our heads in disbelief. Some places would send us off with prayers and a pizza for the road. We were extremely grateful for this! Other places would take up an unsolicited offering in a baseball hat and fill our pockets with money. Those nights left us in tears and with enough money to cover our gas, hotels, and food for the next week. We were absolutely overjoyed whether we received prayers, pizza, money, or nothing at all—we were there for something far more valuable than money.

———

A few months into this journey, I began to feel worn out. Amidst all the busyness and our hectic schedule, it had been awhile since I really heard the voice of God clearly. That left a void that was filled with other thoughts, input, and noises that empowered lies of deception in my mind. Questions and doubts filled my head about how sustainable this whole journey really was. How long could we keep doing this? How could we have kids and invite them into this craziness?

Then, one night in Forth Worth, Texas, God showed up and dispelled all my doubts in one fell swoop. We were in the middle of an all-night Burn gathering. We brought our sleeping bags in with us that night and were planning to just sleep in the prayer room. I had to take a worship set in the middle of the night and we did not have a place to stay.

The day before, I began to question our reason for stepping out on this journey. I wondered if we were even changing anything with all our worship and prayer. I knew that every time we gathered, God was faithful to show up. But for some reason, I thought we would be further along by that point. The romantic life of a road warrior had faded and I was tired of sleeping on hard and dusty floors in random places. I was over eating pizza and pasta every single night. I was sick of long drives. I was done.

As I took time in the prayer room the next night to process and lament to the Lord about why He had led us down this road, I began to question if it was even Him who called us. Maybe we had done this all in the flesh because we thought it was a good idea. Maybe we should have listened to our friends, our parents, and people smarter and wiser than us. Maybe it was all just some crazy dream that was going to crash and burn in front of our eyes.

I also felt really guilty for being a bad husband. After all the work I had done to prepare my life, home, and job for my wife, we were devoting our lives to a room of fewer than twenty people with a horrible sound system and a musty odor. We were worshiping and praying together with passion and fervor as if the future of the nations were at stake. I was about to lead a worship set in the middle of the night and did not even know if I believed a single thing about what I was going to sing. Meanwhile, my beautiful bride was lying over in the corner, curled up in her sleeping bag, on a dusty floor.

I silently shouted to God, "I need a revelation of what is happening right now! I don't think I can really continue in this madness unless I see that we are actually bringing a change to the world in some way." Then, as I sat there alone with God, I said, "Do you even care, God?"

Immediately, I entered into an open vision. It was eerily similar to what I had seen when I was a teenager standing on the National Mall in DC. I saw the hand of the Lord holding the entire earth in His palm. I could almost see the seven billion people scattered across every continent. From my perspective, I could see the wars, plagues, disease, sickness, sin, and darkness that covered the earth. I realized how much was happening that needed God's attention. There was so much pain, tragedy, and hopelessness.

Then I saw the eyes of the Lord burning with an intense and jealous devotion. They were the deepest and most passionate eyes of fire that I could ever imagine. They were consumed with zeal and holiness. I shuddered and almost looked away. But in that moment, I realized those eyes were now fixed on a certain geographical location on the globe. Out of all the problems, strife, and issues around the world that night, His eyes were fixated on our little prayer room in Fort Worth, Texas.

I then heard these words: "You have My attention."

I crumbled to the ground in complete awe and conviction and wept uncontrollably. We had the full, unconditional attention of the Creator in that very moment. Suddenly, every painful sacrifice felt worth it. I surrendered myself to God as I vowed to give Him a million more sleepless nights of worship all across America and the world.

Those burning eyes—that moment—reoriented my theology and realigned my heart. I no longer questioned the power of our prayers or our worship. If we had the gaze and attention of the Almighty, anything was possible.

CHAPTER 8

THE NATIONS

As doors began to open for us in America, the doors to the nations also flung open wider than ever before. We continued to travel from city to city planting furnaces of worship and prayer that prioritized God's Presence, but we also felt our hearts enlarge for the nations of the world.

Kate and I both began having encounters and visions during worship where the faces of unreached people groups—those caught in the sex trade, the marginalized, the war-torn nations—all flashed before our eyes. We had always carried the nations in our hearts, but something shifted rather abruptly for both of us. Reaching the world with the gospel became all that we could think about, talk about, and dream about together.

The countless minutes, hours, and days spent pouring our love, affection, and worship on Jesus began to make sense. The worth of Jesus is enough reason, in and of itself, to continue building altars across the world. We will never reach the end of His worth. That is the foundation of our response to Him. We will never even be able to fully articulate it! The worth of Jesus is why creation groans, the elders bow, and the angels continue to cry out day and night. It is what we were created for and what we will be doing for all of eternity.

Yet, God began to show me something else, as well. The way He releases, reveals, and implements His kingdom is through worship. In the revelation of worship, He directs our hearts, thoughts, and prayers to burn for the things He burns for. That is what the incense was for in the Temple. It represented the revelation of the knowledge of Jesus Christ spreading like lightning across the earth! The deeper we go into His heart, the more we understand His purposes.

The commissioning of Isaiah gives us a peek into this truth.

> In the year that King Uzziah died, I saw the Lord, high and exalted, seated on a throne; and the train of his robe filled the temple. Above him were seraphim, each with six wings: With two wings they covered their faces, with two they covered their feet, and with two they were flying. And they were calling to one another:
>
> "Holy, holy, holy is the Lord Almighty;
> the whole earth is full of his glory."
>
> At the sound of their voices the doorposts and thresholds shook and the temple was filled with smoke.
>
> "Woe to me!" I cried. "I am ruined! For I am a man of unclean lips, and I live among a people of unclean lips, and my eyes have seen the King, the Lord Almighty."

Then one of the seraphim flew to me with a live coal in his
hand, which he had taken with tongs from the altar. With
it he touched my mouth and said, "See, this has touched
your lips; your guilt is taken away and your sin atoned for."

Then I heard the voice of the Lord saying, "Whom shall I
send? And who will go for us?"

And I said, "Here am I. Send me!"

Isaiah 6:1-8 (NIV)

The Lord revealed three things to me through this passage. The entire
nation was in turmoil because their great king had tragically died, ushering
in a season of mourning, pain, and uncertainty. Isaiah, however, pressed in
deeper to find the greater reality of what was going on. He was not content
with the narrative of loss and uncertainty. He needed to see from a kingdom perspective. We were experiencing the same thing in our times of
worship—God was revealing kingdom perspective as we pressed in to Him.

The second revelation was that heaven is an intensely freaky place to
be. It is clear that Isaiah could barely describe the creatures that are buzz-
ing around the throne of God. They seem to consist of eyes and wings and
they are singing antiphonally about the nations being full of His glory. In
the midst of Isaiah's darkest hour and hardship for his people, he heard
heaven singing about how there is still glory to be found in the brokenness
of humanity. I absolutely love this perspective!

The last revelation I experienced came from Isaiah's response to God:
he was completely undone by God's glory, revealing the extravagant depths
of his own dysfunction and sin. This is what the Presence of God does
in our lives. We are convicted of our compromise and simultaneously
reminded of our potential. Once God released forgiveness for Isaiah's sins,
He pulled back the veil of His heart and allowed Isaiah to be privy to His

deepest desire: the nations. This entire wild encounter with the beautiful glory and Presence of God resulted in Isaiah's commission to the nations of the world. I felt that same sense of being sent—commissioned by God—during that season.

———

It was past midnight, somewhere in East Texas, when Kate had a powerful vision during worship. She saw a woman trapped in the sex trade and decided to paint a picture of her. She wrote the words "For the Silent" over the mouth of the girl in her painting. As she prayed, Kate was caught up in weeping and travail for the millions around the world trapped, with no way out. God imparted to Kate His heart of compassion, pain, desire, and hope for His daughters who were having their innocence stolen at such a young age.

The very next day, Kate received an email from someone who had dreamed of her the night before. In the dream, this individual saw Kate becoming "a voice for the silent." Her heart burned when she read that email and a new passion was lit. Kate became determined to bring awareness and change to the horrible injustices taking place in many nations around the world. She joined up with several other people who carried the same burden and they began to plan and mobilize for a marathon that would raise money for that cause. The next week, through a divine connection, she found a local organization named "For the Silent" with the exact same, heart, purpose, and passion that God was speaking to her.

Nearly every day, we had dreams, visions, or confirmations that reinforced our call to the nations. Although we hadn't traveled overseas together since our honeymoon, we could feel our hearts enlarging for the world. During that season, every night when I closed my eyes to sleep, I saw a picture of my room in high school, with one entire wall filled with a giant map of the world. I remembered my dedication to those five nations written on the sticky note posted on my wall. The golden thread God was weaving was finally starting to make sense.

The moment of activation came late one night during a worship gathering. A woman began praying for the billions of Muslims around the world to encounter the love of God. We had prayed these prayers many times before, but I could feel a weight on this one. My heart began to beat fast with expectation. In order to focus our prayers, we compiled a list of the largest Muslim nations in the world according to their population. To my surprise, and probably the surprise of many in the room, Indonesia was number one on that list. Two hundred fifty million Muslims lived scattered across those islands. As we began praying over that list of nations, I couldn't seem to move on from Indonesia. I was focused on that nation, and even felt physically stuck, as if my feet were in concrete. I knew the Holy Spirit was highlighting something to me.

I had once visited Bali for a few days during a crazy around-the-world trip I took while in college. My dad was also among the first wave of doctors to hit the ground after the catastrophic Banda Aceh earthquake and tsunami in 2004 that killed nearly 200,000 people. He told me the stories about how open the hearts of the people were to receive Jesus in what was once known as "Little Mecca." At the same time, I did not necessarily feel called to go back there.

As we prayed, I had a vision of a dark man holding a rod shaped like the island chain of Indonesia. Because of his grip on Indonesia, he had complete and total control over the direction of the nation. He could twist it one way or turn it the other.

The moment we began praying, worshiping, and declaring in the prayer room, I saw his grip begin to loosen. The dark figure could not hold the nation as tightly and did not have total control. As the frequency and the volume of our songs and prayers increased, he no longer had control and his grip loosened entirely. I realized, then, that worship would be the key to release breakthrough and freedom over the people living in the largest Muslim nation on Earth. It would also cause a massive ripple effect in the Muslim community worldwide as they would begin to see Jesus for who He really is, turning their hearts to Him.

I left that meeting with a strong sense that we needed to respond by taking a team of worshipers to Indonesia. I felt an urgency and knew we needed to take action quickly.

———

It felt normal for me to lead mission trips and pioneer experiences for people to meet God in the nations. Almost every year since high school, I had led small teams of people with me on this type of trip. One summer in college, I convinced a few friends to go to India and Nepal on a several-week trip. We hired small Tibetan horses to smuggle Bibles into the most remote villages in the Himalayas. Our goal was to reach Tibetan Buddhists who had never heard the name of Jesus before.

Despite how natural it felt, I hadn't led a trip in several years. My drive to lead overseas trips seemed to die, along with my passion for church ministry, after my experience in Tulsa. Not only that, but pioneering the real estate venture had been incredibly time consuming.

Yet, just as He had revived my passion for worship, God was resurrecting my dream to go to the nations, and it seemed to come at the perfect time. As I prayed about the trip to Indonesia, one by one names and faces of people who were going to join me on the trip flashed before my eyes. I believed God was going to handpick the most epic team for this adventure.

The favor on every detail of that initiative was undeniable. Every single person to whom I reached out about joining the team responded with an emphatic YES. It was a divine miracle because the timeline for planning the trip was incredibly short. Everyone needed to get time off of work and raise significant funds in order to go. God showed up in profound ways and met every single person's financial deadlines for the trip. This was going to be our first ever mission trip with The Burn!

Within a matter of a week, we had mobilized a team of thirty fiery lovers of God from all across America! We were ready to bombard the nation of Indonesia with love, compassion, and worship. It was one of the most wild, chaotic, exhausting, and fulfilling trips that I had ever been part of. We hosted a twenty-four-hour nonstop Burn in a massive church building in the city of Despansar. Over 3,000 people streamed in from across Indonesia to attend, and many hundreds stayed through the entire night as we worshiped! God performed many incredible miracles, salvations, and healings on that trip as we held outreaches across the island. The team was an absolute dream and carried such a grace for the wild and jam-packed schedule I put together.

The greatest miracle of that trip may have been what God was doing in my heart. The weariness of life on the road and the disappointment and burden from our horrible experience with the church in Tulsa was finally fading. I felt lighter, more hopeful, and filled with expectation for all God was about to do. The vision I received over ten years earlier while praying on the National Mall felt like it was finally gaining momentum. I was experiencing the "fires" burning in the largest Muslim nation on Earth!

I laid awake many nights in Indonesia, completely undone by God's faithfulness. The fact that my wife was willing to get on a plane and leave America was living proof of it! She overcame her fears of traveling and resisted the thoughts of another failed missions experience so that she could pursue God's heart for the nations. It was our time in Indonesia that allowed us to finally feel in sync once more and in tune with our calling to the nations.

After that trip, my heart was on fire to do more. When we returned home, I recruited anyone and everyone to join me on future trips. Every time I spoke or preached, my message was about taking the movement of worship and prayer and spreading it across the world.

We were experiencing the fullness of Amos 9:11-13, new wine flowing and the promised restoration of the Tabernacle of David. What was happening around us was not another cool worship movement, with better music or a modern logo. Every time we gathered to pray and worship, it was all unto the salvation of the nations. It was upper-room holy moments leading to the gospel being preached and miracles being performed. Our hearts were wrecked with this reality.

We felt emboldened to carry the mandate to target the hardest and the darkest nations on the globe. I recruited a team that would commit one year to sow their lives into Indonesia to keep the fire burning. But we were called to other nations, as well. I remember laying a map on our prayer room floor while scouring the continents and nations we were called to. We focused our attention on Turkey, Iraq, China, India, and the war-torn nations of East Africa.

We had no intention of chasing danger, but Kate and I knew the places we were called to go were unstable and there would always be an element of risk involved. I grew up hearing the glory stories and the horror stories of missionaries all over the world experiencing persecution. While we probably carried a slight notion that we were young and bulletproof, I was laser focused on conflict nations and nothing would stand in the way of our calling.

———

Not long after we returned from Indonesia, God opened a door for us to bring a team to the border region of Uganda and Kenya. For years, this area had been known for turmoil, war, disease, famine, and poverty. But we believed that the Presence of God could bring hope, life, and healing to any situation. This felt like the perfect place to test that theology in real time. Kate opted to stay home and prayed for our team every day as I sent her updates.

The trip went well until our final day in the country. We were in the sprawling Ugandan capital of Kampala. I was exhausted and downright delusional after traveling for thirty-six hours by bus through the East African nations of Burundi, Rwanda, and Uganda. It was disgustingly hot and dusty, and the non-air-conditioned bus ride from Bujumbura to Kampala was littered with border delays, winding mountain roads, car wrecks, and classic African interruptions. It seems nothing goes as planned on that side of the planet.

Despite our physical exhaustion, our team was riding on a spiritual high from the previous two weeks of incredible breakthrough across the region. It felt like Paul's description in 2 Corinthians 12:3: we didn't know if we were in or out of the body! We had witnessed terminal diseases healed, Muslims and Hindus radically saved, countless hearts ignited, and worship and prayer communities birthed. We were exhausted but also filled with joy.

We arrived in Kampala twelve hours later than planned, and then took a two-hour taxi ride to get from the bus station to the house where we would sleep before our early morning flight home. As we were bringing the last load of luggage from the taxi into the house, three men appeared out of nowhere and shoved us through the door, driving the butts of their AK-47 assault rifles into our backs. They threw us to the ground and yelled at us in Swahili, demanding our money, passports, and any valuables. They repeatedly kicked and beat us, pressing the barrels of their loaded guns against our skulls, grinding our faces into the hard cement floor.

We discovered they had followed us since we got off the bus in Kampala just a few hours before. They claimed they were going to "rob, torture, and kill the American." In the crime-infested terrain of East Africa, almost all thieves kill their victims so they cannot be identified after their crime.

Memories from the previous year flooded my mind and heart. *This could be it*, I thought. *This could be the end*. The fact that we did not have much money (as it was the end of the trip) and they could not find my passport (hidden in a secret pocket) made them even more agitated. They continued shouting threats against us while scattering our belongings across the house.

As they pillaged through our luggage, they discovered numerous Bibles and overtly Christian books. They turned to us, as we lay subdued on the ground, and screamed, "Are you followers of The Way?" *Here we go*, I thought. This was the scenario and the very question that we thought we would never face. Yet, it is also the very question every believer faces as we contemplate our personal loyalty to Jesus. Would we stand up in defiant courage and face death for our Savior? Or would we be cowardly and shrink back and deny Him? This was my question. This was my test. This was my reality in that moment.

Something took place in my spirit that I cannot explain. The implications of my answer bypassed the critical thinking of my mind and the inner roaring zeal of my heart exploded with an emphatic answer: "YES! I am a follower of Jesus! YES!" Two times they demanded an answer to the same question. Two times I responded with a resounding yes. Silence filled the room. I waited for the sound of a bullet down the barrel of the gun.

Thousands of miles away, Kate suddenly woke up in the middle of the night. She was awakened by a dream that I was lying naked on a concrete floor with a gunshot wound to the head. That was all that she saw in the dream. It was quick, gruesome, and immediately filled her with panic and fear. She checked her phone to see if I had emailed her an update, but there were no messages. So she began interceding for my life. They were not timid or polite prayers. They were wild, emotional, and exhausting—she somehow knew she was fighting for my life in that moment. After an hour of fervent prayer, she was so weary that she fell back asleep.

Lying on the floor in Uganda, waiting for the gunshot, I suddenly couldn't stop the flood of zeal that was released in my spirit. It was as if the gates of a dam that had been holding back my passion broke open. Praise, worship, and my prayer language flooded out of my mouth like a river! My personal love for Jesus, that I had been stewarding internally my entire life, instantly manifested. Then, we all began worshiping, praying, and boisterously lifting our prayer languages to heaven. The Presence of God filled the room so profoundly that we hardly noticed as our armed captors slipped out of the room and vanished!

I don't know whether those thieves saw giant angels standing in our midst, became threatened in that moment, or were simply freaked out at our boisterous response. But I firmly believe that God saved our lives that day.

Kate woke up the following morning to an email from me with the subject line "ROBBED AT GUNPOINT IN UGANDA!" That moment, that experience embedded a truth in our hearts that cannot be shaken: prayer and intercession are powerful to thwart the plans of the enemy. Just like my vision in the prayer room, I knew without any doubt that we had the full attention of the Lord.

CHAPTER 9

THE MORAVIAN DREAM

We had spent over a year on the road not just hosting one-time worship events but also planting communities that were coming together once or twice per month to host twenty-four, forty-eight, and even up to a hundred hours of nonstop worship. The Burn movement was growing and it was becoming increasingly clear that we needed to create a home base. Living out of our car was no longer productive or efficient. The Burn furnaces that we helped launch while living on the road needed a model community that represented and fully embodied the collision of worship and missions.

We also needed to officially set up a non-profit organizational structure. We couldn't put "1998 black Toyota Camry" as the residence on the federal IRS non-profit application—we needed an address and a team of volunteers who could help us build a framework and administration for the movement.

There were so many amazing cities and communities to choose from, so we began praying about where we should land. There were some great opportunities that came streaming in from across America but we needed to hear the voice of the Lord to confirm where we were called to be. I felt the weight of that decision; it would establish our foundation and chart a course for many years to come.

———

Even though I was still young, I had begun to recognize how God truly works in mysterious ways. Not long before our trip to Indonesia, we had the most unusual encounter—one that could have only been the hand of God—with a new church community. At the beginning of our journey to take Burn to churches and communities across the country, all of our invitations were random. But I paid special attention to a request from a community based at a Church of Christ in Dallas, Texas.

Before I responded to their invitation, I did a little research on the Church of Christ and what they believe. Our heart was for unity and we never really focused on the denominational theology of a specific church, but this was our first request from a Church of Christ. In fact, "Tulsarusalem" had every kind of church under the sun, so I was also curious as to why we hadn't crossed paths with the Church of Christ before. I then discovered why: they have a theology that is strongly against using music in their corporate expression of worship. I could barely believe what I was reading! I sat in a coffee shop researching and kept squinting at the screen over and over again. Why in the world would a church that does not believe in music want to invite The Burn (a musical worship movement) to host an event? It was so strange and intriguing that I knew it could only be God. Well, it definitely was.

As we pulled up to the church to meet some of the leaders, that was one of the first questions out of my mouth. I tried to be more tactful, but I could not wrap my brain around how we were about to host twenty-four hours of nonstop worship in a church that professed a unified stance against using music. They laughed and gently explained how theirs was a far more "progressive" church in the movement. They hosted traditional, conservative services without music, as well as music-led worship services. But what really captured my heart was how God was moving in their midst. They were hungry for the Presence of God.

The church had never hosted anything like Burn before, but they felt from God that it was the moment to introduce it to their people. They were wide-eyed, open-hearted, and expectant for the Holy Spirit to come and do whatever He wanted. Kate and I instantly felt like these people were family.

One of the church staff members and our host, Michael Miller, became our fast friend. He was great at helping newcomers know what to expect when they entered The Burn to worship and pray. "It is like walking into God's living room," he'd say.

During that first worship event, we witnessed the power of God move like I had rarely felt before. The hunger in the room was palpable. It felt like a merging of my youth group revival days mixed with the college dorm room intimacy, and topped off with the longing for a fresh touch of the supernatural.

I drove away from that meeting knowing that one day we would join forces with them in Dallas.

———

When it came time to choose a home base, our hearts were drawn to Dallas and the Church of Christ community we had been building relationship with. Not only did we love their passion for more of God and their growing experience of freedom from religion, but they also had many incredible resources in their community. We would get to know many wise businessmen and women who loved God and who understood how to start and fund organizations and non-profits. This was the missing piece that we needed.

We slowly began to create a home base in that community and started doing life together with our new friends. For a few months we bounced around, living at different people's homes in the region, while we continued to travel and host monthly Burn events. Everyone who had a spare room, garage, or couch made room for us. It was beautiful, uncomfortable, and messy, but it gave us some sense of stability amidst the exploding season of growth. It also allowed us time to explore the massive Dallas-Fort Wort metroplex and decide which area we wanted to call home.

Kate longed to go back to school and finish her degree. She had started at community college back in Virginia and had continued sporadically in Tulsa. She wanted to become the first person in her family to finish college and earn a degree. She felt this was a hurdle she wanted to overcome and I was 100% behind her. But she also wanted to utilize the skills she would learn to join the movement to end sex trafficking across the world. She started researching the degrees that would give her the skills to do this with excellence and precision. Eventually, she enrolled at the University of Texas at Dallas and we found a quaint and affordable home in Richardson, near the school.

After months of living on the road, we finally had a home again! Kate dove headfirst into nesting mode for the first time in our marriage, and her desire to create a family began to grow. That actually may be quite the understatement. She wanted babies, now! Meanwhile, I was working overtime on setting up the organization and building a structure to sustain and grow all that God had been doing. With the help of some amazing and generous people, we finally formed our new non-profit and called it Burn 24-7. The name "Burn" was apparently already used by some cult organization in Texas! We added the "24-7" to help differentiate and because our heart truly was to see nonstop adoration to Jesus take root in every city on Earth.

There was also a dream deep down in my heart that this was the exact people and place where God was going to birth a modern-day Moravian-type community. The Moravians lived in Herrnhut, Germany, and hosted over a hundred years of nonstop prayer without even meaning to do it. The fire of worship and prayer then lead them into one of the greatest missionary movements the world has ever seen. They even built their own coffins to bring with them as they launched out to unreached people groups. John Wesley experienced salvation on a ship in the middle of the Atlantic as he watched a group of Moravians pray through the storm. Later, as he worshiped with some Moravians back in London, his heart was "strangely warmed." He was never the same again.

I desperately desired to see that happen in my generation. *Could this be the beginning of another movement like the Moravians?* I wondered. I was hopeful, idealistic, and expectant that God had called us to do this in Dallas.

A core group of men and women began to gather together and dream over this very concept. We began to do life together. We broke bread together. We prayed together. We wept together. There was an acceleration and a grace of momentum over our lives. It was as though God was establishing decades of spiritual and relational history with people we had only known for a few months.

As a group, we began hosting monthly meetings on Sunday near the

DFW airport. Although the North Texas region was saturated with ministries and churches, something fresh and new was taking place every time we came together. God was building a community to house the fire of the Burn movement. We had a small staff and committed leaders. We did not care about labels or titles but deferred to the grace on each other's lives. It was organic and very different from the top-down hierarchal structures many of us experienced in church.

———

In the midst of radical growth in the movement, Kate and I were personally battling through the pain of infertility. She had finally won me over and I was ready to have kids, only to discover that she could not get pregnant. We expected it to take time to get pregnant, but after a year, we were feeling discouraged. Every month, Kate would take a pregnancy test. When she saw the results, she would break down in tears, and we would have to pull ourselves together before the next meeting, gathering, or trip.

I tried to compartmentalize the drama of it all and assure her that it was going to happen in God's perfect timing. But her heart ached more than I had ever seen in our few years of marriage. She wanted a family more than anything in the world. It was difficult to dream and plan for a Moravian-style community in the midst of our hope deferred.

One night, Kate was taking a shower after her college classes when she experienced a wild vision. She saw herself walking across a dusty plain, with white tents everywhere. She knew it was somewhere in the Middle East. She reached down to pick up one of our children, and then, suddenly, the vision was gone and she realized she was at home, in Dallas. She heard the voice of God say, "Do not let your own fear hold your children back from the calling on their lives to the nations."

In that moment, the floodgates of her inner turmoil were released and she began to weep uncontrollably. Kate had a massive fear of the Middle East, and she believed the vision was speaking directly to that fear. With every sob, she allowed her heart to release control of her children to the Lord. These children had not even been born yet! That vision, however, restored hope in our hearts that we would have children and that they would belong to the Lord all the days of their lives. The complete fulfillment of that vision would not come to pass until many years later.

———

The energy continued to surge on our Moravian community plant, but after a few years, tensions also began to bubble up. The Burn 24-7 movement demanded regular national and international travel. I was not present as much as I would have liked, but I also carried the weight of the financial demands of the movement. I needed to host events, conferences, and fundraisers to keep everything going. The other core leaders were also stretched thin with family and work issues beyond what we could manage. What began with consistency and intentionality soon started fragmenting and falling apart.

Our relationships and connection with one another began to rapidly deteriorate as a result. There seemed to be many reasons for this. It was nearly impossible to coordinate our schedules between travel, work, and the sheer distance we lived apart from each other. The nightmare of Dallas-Fort Worth traffic only brought more challenges to our situation. Rumors and accusations started swirling and offenses starting to stick. A cloud of warfare, that we didn't even recognize at the time, hung over our personal lives, marriages, and relationships. I knew the enemy was actively engaged to thwart the dreams God had given us.

Kate and I both felt like we were on the outside looking in within a matter of months. The dream that had brought us to Dallas was slipping away before our eyes. I could not understand what was happening or why—all I knew was that it felt unsettling. I do not like to give the devil tons of credit for our own dysfunctions, but this felt like it had his fingerprints all over it.

We were on the verge of creating a new prototype of church, a house centered on the DNA of the Burn movement. Instead, we decided to pause our monthly gatherings and weekly leadership meetings to reassess the future of Burn 24-7 and our dream of building a Moravian community.

As the growth around the world continued, the dream of building a home base was at a total standstill. Instead of living in that frustration, I threw myself into the global missions side of the movement and traveled more than ever before. We still couldn't get pregnant. We felt alone, isolated, and confused. Kate and I knew we needed a family—fathers and mothers. We started to pray, seek, and actively look for locations to transition to that could provide this.

It seemed like all the pieces, dreams, and personnel were in place to build in Dallas, but the timing was way off. I knew that the seeds we had sown in Dallas for the past three years would bear fruit, but I also felt it was time to move on.

I'm not sure whether any of us knew at the time what the fulfillment of the dream would look like. The fullness of this vision was established when the church, Upper Room, was birthed in Dallas a few years later. It was the culmination of our dream from the beginning—a true praying, worshiping, missional, and Moravian community.

This community has now blossomed to become one of my favorite new God expressions in the world. God's hands were all over it from the beginning, but none of us were ready or correctly positioned with the dedication and leadership skills needed for the fullness of the dream to come forth. Although it was painful to leave before the dream was fulfilled, we knew the seed God called us to sow would one day yield a harvest.

So neither the one who plants nor the one who waters is anything, but only God, who makes things grow.

1 Corinthians 3:7

CHAPTER 10

OVERCOMING LOSS

The whispers of transition in our hearts grew louder and louder, and I began to feel way in over my head in most areas of my life. The Burn 24-7 movement had grown exponentially around the world and we were grasping at structural models as we tried to resource it. The size and scope were already far bigger than we had imagined. A seemingly random network of burning hearts was arising from all corners of the earth. It was like they were coming out of their season of hiding, receiving activation, and then mobilizing day and night worship like never before.

Every new Burn leader carried a unique story of how our paths crossed and worlds collided. None of it happened through social media or online resources. We weren't using any of those tools at that point. Every connection was almost exclusively and divinely God and Holy Spirit happenstance. The leaders were diverse in age, race, class, and location, but they all carried the same heart for the Presence of God.

We would typically launch Burn at a new location by organizing twelve, twenty-four, or even forty-eight hours of nonstop worship and prayer during our initial visit. The community would continue to fan these flames at least once and sometimes twice per month while connecting with our regional and global leaders for conference calls, summits, and various trainings. I would do my best to visit each community at least once per year. So many new furnaces were being planted that it soon was difficult to visit each one every year.

As grateful as I was for this movement, the growth was also painful. I was more aware than ever of my own lack as a leader. My gifting and abilities were stretched thin and my capacity to give was maxed out. The relational strain was especially difficult. I was not able to be as accessible to everyone as I once was. This caused tension with some close friends who felt we were more connected in function than in friendship. My desire was always to build family and connection, but the bigger things became, the harder it was to maintain the depth of relationship I desired to have with every single person. It was impossible.

———

We prayed constantly about where God was leading us to go in our transition from Dallas. At one point, our prayers turned toward Kona, Hawaii—a significant place for both me and Kate. Besides that, we would be pioneering curriculum at a new YWAM school based in Kona. The curriculum, called "Fire and Fragrance," was a collaboration with our good friend Andy Byrd. Andy and I both believed God was bringing a collision of the worship and prayer movement to the missions movement. The fire of worship and prayer would become a fragrance of missions to change even the darkest corners of the world. The school would be our new training arm for world missions, and the Kona YWAM base would provide a test run. Surely things were lining up for us to move there?

Yet, God continued to emphasize our need to surround ourselves with fathers and mothers. This theme continued to hunt us down while we prayed about our next move. I had many fatherly figures in my life who I had connected with over the years. We ran into each other at events and I would call them at times when I was in a bind or to ask for advice. But I had never actually lived in the same community on a daily basis with a spiritual father. The Lord, as usual, was guiding our steps.

Kate and I were in Israel for a massive gathering of worship and prayer that thousands of Jews, Arabs, Russians, Europeans, Americans, and more were attending in Jerusalem. Due to threats directed at the event and Israel in general, security was incredibly tight. We arrived late and the doors to the venue were already closed. Kate and I were forced to wait in a little room outside the main hall while security verified our guest passes.

As we waited, I noticed an older pastor sitting across from us who may have been the most joyful human being I had ever seen. He had such a familiar face that I was certain I had seen him in a dream or something. His name was Charles Stock.

We started a conversation with Charles and learned that he was a speaker at the event. He had just gotten off the plane and was also prevented from going in. He was waiting to figure out how to get into the auditorium before his time slot to speak. Despite his exhaustion, the language barrier with the security guards, and the mass disorganization around where we were supposed to be, he just smiled and laughed through the chaos. We sat together sharing our hearts while we waited.

The tone of his voice and the lightness of his eyes changed the entire atmosphere in that crazy situation that day. I looked over at Kate and said, "My new life goal is be that happy and joyful when I am his age!" From that day forward, our relationship began to grow. Charles made himself available to me in that season of transition and encouraged and supported us without ever being controlling. This caused me to trust, love, and honor him even more.

One night, while praying about where we were called to move, I saw a picture in my mind of Charles smiling and heard this phrase from the Holy Spirit: "Surround yourself with joyful fathers in this season!" I knew in that moment we were going to leave Dallas and land with Charles Stock. He lived in Harrisburg, Pennsylvania. It felt incredibly random at the time, but it also felt right. Pennsylvania was not on the short list of places we were praying about moving to. It wasn't even on my list of places that I would ever want to live. But God had a plan and dream of His own.

When I left Virginia after high school, I was fine with never living back on the East Coast again. It was not in my heart to return. I was done with the flat, hot, crowded cities. My heart ached to go back west and to the mountains. I was born in Montana and something about that place kept calling my name. As John Muir once said, "The mountains are calling and I must go." But for whatever reason, God was calling us east.

Our final fleece to confirm it was time to leave Dallas was to sell our home quickly and for our list price. I joked with Kate and bought a "For Sale By Owner" sign at Home Depot. I told her that if we sold the house within a week for the list price, we were definitely in God's will. The next morning I put the sign in the yard and got a full cash offer before noon! I guess we had the green light to go to Pennsylvania.

———

We began our transition in the winter of 2009. Due to the decentralized nature of The Burn, we were able to raise up regional leaders that ensured the movement would continue to thrive in the Texas-Oklahoma-Arkansas region while we moved our focus to the Northeast.

Many notable ministries with incredible global perspective and reach were based in the little central Pennsylvanian town of Harrisburg. I began to research, read books, and find out all that I could about our new home. I discovered that Pennsylvania had some significant revival history! In the eighteenth century, the Moravians pioneered prayer and worship communities all over the state. Their eventual goal was to use them as sending centers to propel missionaries to the nations of the world. I also learned that the founder of the state, William Penn, desired to build a "holy experiment" and his democratic principles became the bedrock on which the US Constitution was written.

I was already excited about the things I was learning when I discovered that Pennsylvania is called the "Keystone State." The word "keys" has been a theme in the prophetic words given to us for a long time (Isaiah 22:22). Kate and I believed that God was giving us keys in Pennsylvania to unlock doors across the world.

At the same time, Kate heard God say that He was establishing a resting place for us after coming out of a season of absolute insanity. We were leaving Dallas pretty tired and a little beat up. She began to look up the history of the town of Harrisburg and the river that ran through it. The banks of the Susquehanna River, where the town is now located, were called "Peixtin" or "Paxtang" by the Native Americans. It was known as a "resting place" or crossroads for travelers.

Our new home felt like it was ripe with promise. While God was graciously providing rest, we were also in a season of rapid expansion and favor. Not only expansion in ministry—we were now traveling 200,000 miles per year to over thirty nations—but an expansion of our family as well. Kate was finally pregnant! Our bout with infertility had ended and she was carrying a literal promise from God into this new season: our little girl.

————

At the start of every year, we organized a Burn 24-7 leaders' fast where we pressed in globally for the word of God and direction for the season. At the beginning of 2010, the main word of direction I received from the Lord was to spend more time with my dad. It felt like such a different word and so practical. After praying over the destiny of nations and asking for strategies for our movement, this was all that I kept hearing every time I prayed. I would see a picture of my dad and feel the urge to be together.

This prompted me to invite my parents to come up and visit us that January and help us get settled into our new place. Our new house was a little Cape Cod-style home built in the 1960s. It was small, cute, had old wooden floors, the utilities were cheap, and the whole house slightly sloped toward the east. It was the perfect place to start a new family.

My parents had never visited our homes in Tulsa or Dallas, so we were excited to finally share this part of our lives with them. During their visit, we carved out an entire day to drive to New York City together and spend time seeing the sites. Having that time together felt like a miracle. As a missions pastor in Virginia, my dad oversaw a vast missions program into dozens of nations. He was extremely busy doing the job of more than five people. Kate and I were also overextended. Apart from running Burn 24-7, I was finishing songs in and out of the studio for a new record that I was recording.

I will never forget that morning we arrived in NYC. The wind was howling and the temperature was at least fifteen degrees colder than Pennsylvania. We immediately bought some classic NYFD winter beanies from a street vendor in Times Square. Then we were off to all the city standards: the Statue of Liberty, "top of the rock" in Rockefeller center, and our favorite pizza spot in the Village. It was the first time I traveled with my dad to a part of the world that I was more familiar with. I felt proud that I was able to finally show him around.

We laughed, shared our latest stories, reminisced, and got lost walking more than a few times throughout the day. It was great, aside from some strange moments with my dad. I noticed him experience random times of fogginess. He would forget simple things throughout conversations that day: names of people, the place we were going to next, or his favorite drink at Starbucks. It was very odd for an extremely sharp man like him. I had never known him to lose his train of thought so much.

On our drive home, he mentioned that he may go in and see a doctor. We both agreed that he was probably just tired from traveling so much and needed some rest and recalibration.

The next week, after my parents drove back to Virginia, I was on a ministry trip to New Zealand. Right before I was about to lead worship at a large outdoor event, I got a call from my dad that still haunts me to this day. He had gone in for a scan because the fogginess in his mind had gotten worse and his headaches began to grow more intense. Over the phone, he told me that they had found a large mass on his brain. They believed it to be a cancerous tumor. Because of the location and the advanced size of the tumor, treatment would need to begin immediately.

After I hung up the phone, I could barely compose myself. There was no way I could go out on stage and lead worship. I ran into the woods and screamed, yelled, and cried out to the Lord. All of the momentum and expectation of that exciting season in our lives came to a screeching halt.

———

As the next few weeks and months began to unfold, I was living in an excruciating paradox. My wife's belly was getting larger and filling with life and the growing promise of God. Simultaneously, my hero, my mentor, and my biggest cheerleader in life was shrinking and fading away from a cancerous tumor.

That season tested every fiber of what I truly believed about God, His goodness, and my faith. My family prayed, fasted, decreed, and worshiped. We collected and organized a book full of prophetic promises and prayers over my dad that expanded daily. He and I would often read them together at night. I would travel to Virginia frequently in those first few weeks and after his brutal chemotherapy treatments, I would play guitar as he tried to recover. All he wanted in that season was to be in the presence of God. We would sit there for hours and hours and he would just ask me to keep playing.

Sometimes, he was so weak, frail, and exhausted by the chemo that he would just sit with a smile on his face, unable to sing or move. Those were some of the most sacred moments of worship. I had never cried so much or felt so broken or in need. But through it all, God's nearness was tangible.

We canceled much of our ministry schedule even as my dad pleaded and begged me to keep going to the nations. He promised that the "threat" of going to heaven did not scare him. He didn't want me to put ministry on hold. In fact, he and I were supposed to go to Iraq together that same year, the next country on my sticky note from my childhood. After he got diagnosed, the first question he asked his doctor was whether or not he could still go with me to Iraq. That revealed just how much he cared about the unreached, the lost, the hurting, and the poor. He also told us, on several occasions, "I just want God to get the glory through all of this, whether He heals me or He does not."

My dad believed with all of his heart that he was going to get healed. No one could convince him otherwise. He woke up every morning and opened his Bible and journal to spend time with the Lord. It was what he had done my entire life, and he never stopped, even in those darkest days.

A breakthrough occurred a few weeks after his diagnosis when he was cleared for surgery at Duke University hospital with the number one brain surgeon in the world. The surgery was successful, but they were very cautiously optimistic. They warned us that the tumor was very aggressive and could show back up again soon. They did believe, however, that surgery would buy us one or two years together. I was very grateful for this!

We traveled between Pennsylvania and Virginia several times each month. My dad randomly called me one day while I was in the studio back in Pennsylvania, trying to finish my album. He wanted to know how the studio process was going and was excited to hear the new songs. He told me over the phone several times how proud he was of me and the man that I had become. He knew how Kate and I were boldly following God's plan, even though it didn't always make sense. He encouraged me that it was really the only way to live. We talked about my next trip to Virginia and I promised I would play him some of my latest songs.

That was the last time I ever talked to my dad.

CHAPTER 11

FATHERHOOD

We had just come up with an album title for my latest project: "Keep this Love Alive." I never truly knew how that title would impact me over the next several months and years. Just a day or two after my phone call with my dad, he woke up in the middle of the night feeling suddenly very sick.

When I received a phone call from my mom that they were headed to the hospital, I jumped in my car and started driving to Virginia. I prayed intensely for the first hour of my drive. Just as I was on the beltway around Washington, DC, my mom called and told me that my dad was gone. He had gone to be with Jesus.

We learned later that he had developed an infection that his weakened immune system could not fight. Just days before, we were celebrating the additional one to two years we were assured to have left, and then he was gone in an instant. He passed away into eternity only three months from his initial diagnosis.

I have never sobbed so deeply in my entire life. The rest of the drive I let out the rawest and most profanity-laced tirade against God that I have ever uttered. I did not even know I was capable of it. I lost my voice before I even reached Virginia.

I arrived at my parents house at 2:00 a.m. and collapsed into my mom's arms. It felt like a nightmare that could not even be possible. None of it made sense. I was so exhausted from sobbing and screaming uncontrollably during my long drive down to Virginia that my body turned off the second my head hit the pillow. That was the last decent night of sleep I would have for a long time.

The next day was otherworldly and surreal. It wasn't just that it felt like the worst dream of my life, but there was an emptiness and hollowness in my soul I can't explain. I was in complete denial of what had taken place. I did not want to get out of bed because that meant I would have to acknowledge my new reality.

Kate was in Tennessee that weekend for her younger sister's wedding. When I had called her the night before with the news, I begged her to stay for the wedding and fly to Virginia afterward. I knew how much that wedding meant to her and the entire family. I didn't want her to miss out on this once-in-a-lifetime moment supporting her sister, and I felt guilty that her sister's special day might be affected.

Kate, however, would not be deterred. In the middle of the night, she bought a plane ticket to Virginia for the first flight out in the morning. She chose to be with me over standing with her sister as the maid of honor. It was one of the most selfless acts of sacrifice anyone had ever done for me. I did not realize until years later how much that decision created a stronger bond between us.

Kate arrived at my mom's house not long after I woke up and immediately ran in to hug me, weeping. I kept saying to her, "I'm so sorry you missed her wedding. I'm so sorry." She told me to never say that again and that she made the right decision to be with me in that moment.

———

The next few days, weeks, and months tested everything I have ever believed, sung, or preached before. I had just finished an entire album of new songs. Now I did not know if I even believed any of them. I was in the middle of co-writing my first book but did not want to release it and actually thought about rewriting much of it. I was truly in a crisis of my soul.

Like most tragic loss that occurs, there was much activity, planning, preparing, and organizing that needed to take place. We had no room to sit back and process. My dad had been the one to take care of everything from finances and car maintenance to lawn care and even the littlest detail of changing air filters in the house. Now my mom was left alone and she had a lot to learn and process.

There were funeral preparations, statements that needed to be made, and life insurance policies to look into. There were debt collection notices and a constant stream of visitors, family, and friends who wanted to pour out their condolences and support for our family. The sheer amount of demand on our time and energy was exhausting and overwhelming. In the midst of all this, Kate and I had a partially renovated home in Pennsylvania that was still strewn with moving boxes. We had spent so little time there since moving that we had barely even engaged locally in our new community. Suddenly, it seemed like we were going to be more based in Virginia for the foreseeable future.

———

The baby in my wife's belly continued to grow. We had decided what to name our baby girl very early on, before my dad got sick. We had no idea how prophetic and timely her name would be to us and everyone in the world affected by my father's passing.

A major theme for us the previous year, in 2009, was the fire of worship and prayer that led to the fragrance of evangelism and salvation. I was preaching many messages solely around this concept. We were also about to launch a ministry school named "Fire and Fragrance."

One of the anchor verses for this theme came out of 2 Corinthians 2:14-16:

> But thanks be to God, who always leads us as captives in Christ's triumphal procession and uses us to spread the aroma of the knowledge of him everywhere. For we are to God the pleasing aroma of Christ among those who are being saved and those who are perishing. To the one we are an aroma that brings death; to the other, an aroma that brings life.

I camped out on the concept of the call of worshipers to walk through the lows and highs of life as a "triumphal procession." It carried the optimism and the expectation that I felt we needed to embody in a world full of uncertainty and chaos. I taught and preached that our lives were a fragrant offering of worship. It was the fragrance of LIFE, hope, joy and peace. It carried something that was often contradictory to our circumstances. We are the "aroma of Christ." When my wife looked deeper into the words "aroma" and "fragrance," we discovered that the Hebrew translation was *Keturah*.

My wife became obsessed with that word as a name. Not only was it incredibly unique to us (we did not know anyone else named that), but it was inherently special to us in that season. Little did we know how much we would need that message, that fragrance, and that baby after the loss of my father.

Often, during the first and second trimester of her pregnancy, Kate would sit on our bed at night and I would finger pick my guitar next to her belly. We would laugh at how Keturah would respond with kicks and movement the moment the guitar strings were plucked. This was even before the books and research said the baby should be able to hear! She was so sensitive to music and immediately responded with movement of praise.

I stopped doing this after my dad passed away. I was not in the head space to even talk or think about the pregnancy, and my baby girl continued to grow with almost zero attention, reflection, or acknowledgment from me. Kate was kind, compassionate, and understanding through it all, allowing me the space I needed to process.

———

I canceled my entire ministry schedule and trips for the coming months not knowing when or if they would ever resume. At that point, I was fine if they never happened. My theology and optimistic view of life were completely annihilated. I lost my desire to trust God. Every prophetic word we received felt like a lie. I lost all desire to sing. It was the first time I felt like there was no reason for living. I could not get on a stage and promote, preach, or sing something I no longer believed in. It was not that I stopped believing in God, but it was His ability to heal and care for the things of my heart that I questioned.

My dad repeatedly reminded us that even if he didn't get healed, there should be no room in our hearts to be offended at God. But I knew there was no one kinder, gentler, more humble, or more deserving of a miracle than my dad. He was the most blameless and meek human I had ever met. And God didn't heal him. I was very offended.

Not only was I empty and angry, but I began to feel alone in my process. It seemed like so many of my friends and even my family resorted to clichés and "refrigerator magnet" Bible verses to cope with the devastation of my dad's passing. I don't blame them at all—that is what most people do. It is how we are taught, as Christians, to respond to negative experiences.

But at the same time, that response felt inauthentic and frustrating to me.

I am not saying that those around me didn't authentically believe those verses or phrases—and maybe for some of them, it brought peace. None of us had answers for why my dad was gone, especially after how hard we had prayed, fasted, and believed for a miracle. I had mobilized thousands around the world via social media to press in, pray, and believe with us. For me, however, the familiar Christian response wasn't enough. I despised anyone even smiling, recollecting funny jokes, or bringing any light-hearted nature in the room. I dove headfirst into the inescapable question raging through my mind: Why did God allow him to die?

I did not want easy answers to my questions, either. Instead, I needed lasting, deep understanding. And I knew that I either needed to face the noise of my swirling soul right then and there, or it would fester and become a source of constant pain, offense, and brokenness in the days and years to come. I had known people who shoved down these difficult feelings. They escaped the questions because it seemed more convenient at the time. I could empathize with them because it probably was. But their inability to deal with pain became a wound that grew and festered and eventually derailed their faith.

I knew all the verses and theology that were meant to bring us comfort. Heaven has no cancer, pain, or hardship. My dad was clearly in a much better place. But what about us? What about my mom, who was suddenly a widow, forced to pick up the pieces of her broken life? My theology brought no comfort or solace in that moment. He died too soon, way too soon. His tumor had been removed—just weeks earlier we had celebrated the fact that the tumor had not grown back quickly, like they predicted it would. I thought we were living in a miracle. Instead, my dad succumbed to a casual sickness that his body would have easily fought off if he hadn't been so weak from the chemotherapy. That was not how his story was supposed to end. We were robbed. He would never even meet his first grandchild. It was a senseless tragedy. There were no clean or tidy explanations that could cure the grieving in my soul.

The only freeing thing in my heart at the time was that I did not feel rushed to find answers. I dove into my own personal wrestle with God not knowing when I would find resolve. I felt completely wounded and let down by the Lord. He abandoned my family when we needed Him most. My mom was left without a husband, my sisters and I were left without a father, and hundreds of missionaries around the world were left without a pastor. We did all the right things and made all the right moves when we found out about the tumor. We stood in the face of the diagnosis and worshiped. We remained unshaken in our resolve every single time we prayed. We followed every step that was in the Bible to see a breakthrough come. Yet it did not happen. We had failed, and God had failed us.

My faith was tired. As I began to wrestle with the deeper questions of the goodness of God and His faithfulness toward us, I found some solace in the life of King David. He externally processed his pain, loss, anger, and even resentment of God in the Psalms. The songs of David's life are filled with the most vulnerable, brutal, and oftentimes blasphemous language. He showcased his emotions as he journeyed through the highs and lows of life. It seemed nothing was off limits in the book of Psalms. That is one reason why it is still studied in the most prestigious higher education institutions today. Harvard, Yale, and Cambridge still tout the book of Psalms as one of the most vulnerable and poetic literary works that has ever been written.

I know that God is not afraid of, embarrassed by, or upset with our questions. In fact, He welcomes them. Truly the only way for us to live authentically before an authentic God is to "work out our salvation with fear and trembling" (Philippians 2:12). King David always kept the conversation with God going, and it eventually led to a resolution—even if it wasn't the resolution he wanted. I was hoping my story would be the same.

If I ever was to pick up a guitar or speak publicly again, I would need to find some ground to stand on. Like Jacob in the book of Genesis, I was willing to wrestle and not let go of God until I was wounded at the hip. It was far better to live with a limp the rest of my life and be authentic than fake it and walk straight.

———

I was not only working through my own feelings toward God but I was feeling a flood of emotions toward people around me as well. I was harboring my own expectations of how I felt they should respond. Many people I loved, who had known my family and my dad, kept silent after his passing. Often people do not know how, when, or in what manner to respond when something that devastating happens. So they do and say nothing. Many never called, sent a text, emailed, or engaged in any way. It infuriated me and created distrust toward those people.

In some ways, the support we received came from the most unexpected places, from friends and leaders who were further removed from our story. One of those was Beni Johnson in Redding, California. She invited us to come to a leadership conference at Bethel Church and just receive in that season. Honestly, a church conference was the last place I wanted to go. I was done with church meetings for the time being. In fact, that is what I wanted to run away from until I had something solid in my heart to stand on. But she insisted, saying she heard from the Lord that we were supposed to come. She also wanted me to get some time with her husband, Bill Johnson, who had also lost his father in a similar manner years before.

My wife really believed it was moment for us to heal and would help us get away from the crazy swirl of life in Virginia. She believed it would allow us to reconnect as a couple and free our minds in a new space. We flew to California together a few weeks later.

They were incredibly gracious to us and gave us free tickets to the conference and set up a personal meeting with Bill. I don't remember much of the conference sessions; I don't think we went to many of them. But I do remember the meeting with Bill.

When we walked into his office, he welcomed us with a smile and told us how much he was praying for us through our loss. I fully expected a pretty flow of "tweet-able" statements that would supposedly solve every theological crisis I was facing. That was the very reason I did not want to be there. But that never happened.

Those who have walked through extravagant loss understand that the last thing people need when walking through the dark night of the soul is answers. They just need friends. Bill knew how to be a friend in that moment. He also stepped into a fatherly role in our lives. He showed me pictures of his dad on his computer and talked about how much he missed him. He shared how hard it was when he lost his father to cancer and the short timeline they had with him after his diagnosis. It was almost identical to my current situation. He shared his story about how it occurred in a season when he felt the mandate to press into miracles and healings in his own ministry and congregation.

Miracles began to break out in extravagant measures all around him. God was answering the deepest cries of his heart. Then, his dad became sick and tragically died almost three months after the initial diagnosis. It happened very fast and was gut-wrenching for him and the entire congregation. It also went against the supernatural manifestations that were happening in their midst. Just before we finished our conversation, Bill turned to me and said, "If you want to have a peace that passes all understanding through this loss, you must lose your right to understand."

Even though I didn't fully agree in the moment, those words began to sink deep into my heart. In the same way the lives of David and Jacob gave me permission to wrestle and struggle, those words from Bill gave me permission to let it go without coming to a perfect resolution. In the end, it was about my trust in God. Could I release control of understanding why He allowed this to take place and trust Him in the unknown?

———

During this process that lasted several months, the arrival of our baby was closing in. I was desperately trying to get my mind and heart in a place of resolution with my father's death so that I could receive the new life of my daughter.

After putting my guitar down after my dad's death, I didn't know if I was ever going to pick it back up again. The day my daughter was born, however, something inside told me to bring my guitar to the hospital. I had always dreamed of having a little worship time with my family the very first day our baby was born. Despite the turmoil in my heart, I wasn't going to sacrifice the opportunity to share that moment with my wife and daughter.

After nineteen hours of natural, intense back labor in the birthing room in Norfolk, Virginia, Keturah Liv Feucht arrived in our arms. It was like heaven opened over us in a moment. As I held her in my arms, I was completely in awe of that absolute miracle. She was our very own "fragrance of life."

I gazed into her eyes and something unexpected happened in my heart. I started to feel the sting of my dad's untimely death melting off of me. Our little fragrance of life was infusing hope into my heart again. I saw the goodness of God in her little toes and fingers and reveled in the beauty of this "rainbow baby." She had become the very thing that I was to my own parents after my brother's death: a restoration of God's faithfulness in our lives.

Less than an hour after she was born, I opened my guitar case and held my guitar for the first time in months. I leaned over the clear plastic hospital cart where Keturah lay and started to strum the guitar. Tears streamed down my face and I was so overcome that I could not even sing a single note. I just strummed and played while I watched her little feet move to the sound of the music.

In that hospital room, staring at my new little baby girl, while basking in the faithfulness of God, I slowly began to get my song back. It was a broken, weak, and frail song, but it was real and it was mine. Healing came to my heart that day and a deep sense of gratitude rose up that displaced my pain and doubt. Our miracle baby was here. God was still good.

CHAPTER 12

MAN OF WAR

When the "fragrance of life" crashed into our lives, she not only helped ease the sting of losing my dad, she also rejuvenated my calling and drive. The world suddenly opened up again and I was able to pull out of the deep hole of despair I found myself in. My dreams started coming alive again and I had found myself thinking about legacy. There was one question I kept asking myself: What did I receive from the life of my father that I could build upon and pass onto my children? That was what I lay awake at night thinking about.

The legacy my father passed onto me was one of global magnitude. He was beloved, cheered on, championed, and then mourned around the world. Videos, pictures, books, memorials, and long messages continued to pour in—even months after his passing—from those moved by his life

across the globe. The pictures alone were mind boggling. One in particular stuck out to me at the time. At the end of a successful and powerful
medical clinic in West Africa, my dad planted a church because so many
villagers had given their lives to Jesus. They had no buildings or structures
to hold the many new converts, so my dad had them meet under a large
tree. They took a picture together standing in front of the tree for my dad
as a tribute. That church still meets there to this day.

My dad often went where no one else was willing to go. He brought
healing, hope, and restoration to the poorest of the poor and weakest of
the weak. I not only wanted to build upon that legacy, but I wanted my
children's children to be part of the story God was writing in our family. I
desired for them to be in on the action themselves—be part of what God
was calling us to—while building a history of adventure with God in the
midst of growing up. Just like my first experience in Brazil gave me insight
into why my dad gave his life to missions, I wanted to pass the same inher-
itance to my children.

A week after Keturah was born, we sent off all of her papers to get her
first US passport. We already had a trip planned in less than two months
and were ready to take our new little family on the road! Australia would
become the first stamp in her passport.

Many friends and leaders in our life warned us that things would be
much slower and more difficult with a baby. They had genuine concern
about the pace of our lives and wanted to temper our expectations. I totally
got it. But for some reason, we felt a grace in that season and especially over
Keturah. She was like an angel when she flew on planes. Good thing too,
as they quickly became her second home. The moment we would take off,
Keturah would go into a deep sleep. When we arrived in different time
zones and nations, jet lag did not affect her one bit. We started to believe
that was normal for all babies.

We felt the wind of God over our plans as a family and we began to take her everywhere we went. She fell asleep most nights in an atmosphere of worship. If there was not music, loud talking, or laughter, she would have a hard time sleeping. We were unintentionally training her to go with the flow, sleep wherever we laid her down, and wake up with wide-eyed wonder at the new city, country, and people around her. She absolutely carried wonder!

———

The season we were in could have been titled "The Resurrection of Broken Dreams." Not long after we returned from that first family trip to Australia, I received the most random email from someone I had never met. It was an invitation to be part of a special team to North Korea.

With all the heartache and pain of losing my dad, I had forgotten that sticky note stuck to the wall in my room, listing the five most persecuted countries in the world. It had been many years since the trip to Afghanistan. I quit praying and hoping to see the same thing happen in the other four nations. It was not that I didn't care about them; I just saw no way of ever getting to those nations. There was one country on the list, however, that stood above the rest with regard to impossibility. That was the nation of North Korea.

It was last on my list of places I ever thought I would visit. The only person I knew to visit North Korea was my dad, many years before. He was part of a team that smuggled Bibles into the country and actually spent a night in jail because of it. At this point, Americans were not allowed entry into North Korea, a country that was the number one violator of human rights and exhibited widespread Christian persecution. It was even difficult to get accurate data on what was actually happening in the nation. The few people who defected into South Korea and China, and survived, painted a very grim picture.

The trip I was invited to join would not be publicized and would fall under a new Democratic People's Republic of Korea (DPRK) program inviting foreigners to visit in hopes of changing the perception of the nation. It was an experiment to see if they could appear civil, open-minded, and innovative to the rest of the world. Americans were not normally accepted under the new program, but they had opened a few spots to US citizens for a trial run. The caveat was that everywhere we traveled across the country, we would be accompanied by armed military soldiers watching our every move.

There were absolutely no guarantees on safety, security, or the promise that we would even return. It was probably the last place a new father should run off to just months after his first baby was born! When I finished reading the email, I was convinced there was no way Kate would ever allow me to go. But there was also a haunting reminder in my heart that the trip was the direct answer to my prayers! It must have been God! I waited a few days before telling my wife about the opportunity. I needed more time to process how I would tell her. I waited until right before the deadline to talk to her. I then tried to slip it casually into conversation one day. I don't think I succeeded. "You want to what? Go where? There?!" She screamed, "And leave me with our new baby all by myself?"

I asked her to at least pray and sleep on it that night before I shared more details. I knew it would have to be an act of God for her to ever say yes. She woke up the next day and simply said, "You can go."

Before I could ask questions, she said, "I know you were created to do this and God reminded me of that. I cannot hold you back from this open door." I immediately responded to the email, "YES! I AM IN!" I then began to feel all the feels. Expectation, nervousness, and excitement rose in my heart at the very thought of taking a step off the plane into that nation. God was faithful to answer my prayers from fifteen years earlier, and I was headed to North Korea.

———

It turns out that I knew most of the team members being assembled for this historic trip. Some of them had suggested to the lead organizer that I be invited on the trip as well, which explained the unexpected email. We carried a sobriety and awe of this once-in-a-lifetime experience. We convened in Beijing for a day of briefing and training before taking the flight directly into Pyongyang. I did research on the city and discovered that a massive revival took place in Pyongyang in the early 1900s, a direct effect from the Azusa Street outpouring in Southern California. Bodies were healed, souls were purified, and hearts were saved as a massive wave of God's power crashed over the nation. Many historians believe over one million Koreans were swept into the kingdom during that time. Pyongyang became such a hot spot for the revival that it carried the nickname "the Jerusalem of the East."

There was a story God was writing in that nation and it wasn't finished yet. At the time of my trip, however, the amount of persecution and deaths of Christians was staggering. It was by far the most difficult place on the planet to follow Jesus.

We gathered as a team in the Beijing hotel for a time of worship and prayer the night before our flight to North Korea. As I prayed, my heart shifted from feeling anxious to feeling joyful and giddy. Everything inside of me that was fearful became carefree and hopeful. I could not stop smiling and was even laughing while thinking about getting on the plane to the most closed nation on Earth. The Holy Spirit directed me to this verse: "These I will bring to my holy mountain and give them joy in my house of prayer" (Isaiah 56:7).

The moment our plane landed in Pyongyang, I could sense God's joy over that land. From then on, the angry faces, the intense gestures, the waiving of the guns—none of it fazed me. In fact, our entire team carried such a beautiful lightness as we traveled across the nation. Our goal was to radiate hope in every conversation, every glance, and every open door God provided. Not only were we able to bring guitars, pass out Bibles, and meet fellow believers (all of which was illegal), but we had the privilege of visiting the Korean Demilitarized Zone (DMZ).

The Demilitarized Zone is the most heavily fortified and contested border in the world. It cuts the Korean peninsula into two distinct countries: North Korea and South Korea. Brothers, sisters, daughters, and sons are still separated today by that border. During the bus ride over, I began to feel a song rising up in my spirit that I felt needed to be released there. It was exploding inside me and I could hardly keep it down.

Our team helped me sneak my guitar case off the bus and into the "blue room" in the building along the DMZ. This room straddles the border between North Korea and South Korea. Half is in the north and half in the south. Presidents, prime ministers, dignitaries, and celebrities have worked for decades to broker a treaty for peace and even reunification in that same room. All of their attempts have failed as the two countries officially remain at war.

In a moment ordained by God, we were invited inside that room. Soldiers lined up against the walls as we walked inside. We sat in the same chairs as the world leaders who came before us. We, however, didn't come with an elaborate peace plan and we didn't even know why we were brought there. So we did the only thing we knew to do: we began to pray together and lay hands on the table in front of us.

As if on cue, the soldiers began transitioning out of the room. It seemed like they were on a shift change, so I took advantage of the chaos and reached for my guitar. I began to strum and sing the lyrics to the song that was in my heart:

Faithful to the end,
You will finish what you started.
Oh my God.
You can do anything
Oh my God,
Nothing is too hard for you.

We had just a few minutes of worship before the next group of soldiers entered and immediately motioned for me to stop playing, but the damage was already done. We prayed the prayers and sang the song we were brought there to sing. We believed that may have been the entire reason we were called to visit that nation. There was a prayer or song we needed to release there that would cause things to change. Like Paul and Silas, surrounded by bleak circumstances in prison, the sound of their worship caused the earth to shake and the gates to open! That was our prayer for North Korea. In the very place where delegations and peace discussions had failed, God would make a way.

Thankfully, we were able to leave safely and returned home glowing with the testimonies of God's goodness, grace, and power. Even in the darkest and hardest nation on the earth—boasting an iron-fisted regime seeking to stamp out the gospel—nothing could truly hold back the spread of an unstoppable kingdom.

———

That trip to North Korea lit my heart on fire for closed nations and unreached people groups. I was still engaged with my primary focus on building Burn 24-7 across the world, but there was also a community forming in Pennsylvania that possessed a far more missional heart than any place we had lived.

We had quite an extensive network of leaders we had raised up by this time and many desired to live in closer proximity as we pioneered training schools, outreach initiatives, and carried on the dream of the Moravian community. But I was initially very hesitant to invite other friends and families to move along with us to the Northeast. I was not confident yet of how deep our involvement would be locally in this community or how much we would travel.

But one by one, singles, couples, and families began to move to our town. They actually came from nations all over the world and they all carried the word of God to come. They were missional in their hearts and felt like Pennsylvania was an interim place to get trained and equipped before being sent off to the nations.

Over the next several years, we focused on building day-and-night worship and prayer, training, equipping, inner city work, and outreach to university campuses. We based our ministry out of a massive mansion in the heart of the roughest part of our city. The mansion had been built in the 1800s from the materials left over after the construction of the capitol building. A Mennonite church owned it for years but no longer used it and had let the building fall into disrepair.

Harrisburg was rated one of the worst cities for crime and murder in America. Our first month there, our interns witnessed four murders take place on the streets. We longed to see the principles of consistent worship and prayer change the spiritual atmosphere and climate over the city.

We also caught God's heart for what many called the "cold northeast." We focused specifically on the Ivy League campuses and the cities of New York, Washington, DC, and Boston. We studied the history of the first and second Great Awakenings and how they were birthed on the Ivy League campuses. Many of those schools were started as "ministry schools" to train revivalists.

We believed in redemption for those hallowed and humanistic institutions. It was time to see God win over the hearts of a generation drowning in unbelief, cynicism, and intellectual pride. So we pioneered a "God Is Not Dead" tour on an old baby-blue school bus. We packed it full of worshipers and stopped through the campuses of Harvard, Yale, NYU, and Princeton. The lead producers at MTV approached me on doing an entire series of shows around the phenomenon of college students praying all night. They could not fathom university students forgoing the life of independence and unrestraint to commit themselves in holiness to God.

———

After we started gaining some significant traction on these campuses and cities, God moved our attention back to the nations. By 2013, we felt our hearts being drawn specifically to the Middle East.

Life in Pennsylvania had been full: local and international ministry, building, community, and even growing our family. Our second child, Malachi, was born in 2012. By then, however, several key prophetic words that were given to us when we first moved to Pennsylvania started to become reality. One of those words was from Cindy Jacobs, who was a great friend and spiritual mom in our lives. She prophesied that "the Keystone State would provide the keys to unlock doors in the Middle East."

Up until that point, we had not traveled much to the Middle East. We did not have a ton of connections there, either. But my heart was beginning to enlarge for the billions of Muslims around the world. Kate and I, along with our good friends Holly and Andy Byrd, decided to take a five-week family scouting trip to the Middle East. We had only two children at the time, Keturah and Malachi. They had four! We were all white Americans who only spoke English and stuck out like a sore thumb everywhere we went.

We chose the nation of Turkey as our home base. Turkey has one of the highest concentrations of Muslims in the world while boasting the second most biblical history behind Israel. The people speak very little English but are very welcoming to Westerners. We hoped to visit the thriving Burn 24-7 communities scattered across Turkey. Andy and I also planned a few trips to the surrounding nations and would be gone for a few days each week while the family stayed back.

We experienced incredible favor across the Gulf Nations. Each day was unique as we waited on God to show us where to go, who to talk to, and what to accomplish. Every single day He led us where we needed to go. We felt connected and in love with the people, cultures, and history across the region.

The last few days of the trip, however, brought one of the most vile spiritual attacks against our family we had ever faced. Kate took a prayer walk with a few families and the kids through an unreached village. There were no Christian witnesses established in the entire region of villages. The kids smiled and waived to the villagers as they walked along. Suddenly, an old woman screamed and yelled in Turkish while pointing to Kate and fourteen-month-old Malachi in her arms. Our friend who lived there and spoke Turkish turned to Kate and said, "We need to go. This lady is cursing your baby and saying horrible things."

That night, Malachi had the most severe fever of his life and could not go to sleep. They were in an isolated region of the nation far away from major stores or hospitals. Things started to deteriorate rapidly as the night wore on. His diaper was filling up with blood. Kate was stressing out and had no idea what was happening to him. They rushed him to the nearest hospital right as I was driving back with Andy from another town. The Turkish doctor opened his diaper and immediately began to raise his voice, yelling to his medical staff. They rushed Malachi back for tests and thought something horrible was wrong with him.

The prayer that Kate prayed in the shower years ago in Dallas began to flood back to her mind in that moment. Did she really trust that God was going to keep her children safe? Did she really believe she had released total control of her children to Him?

The reports came back that Malachi had a severe bacterial infection. They hooked him up to an IV and began giving him fluids. They begged us to stay for a few days in Turkey and delay our trip back home to the US. Both Kate and I felt like we needed to get home as soon as we could, not even fully understanding the diagnosis the Turkish doctor had given us. Malachi slowly began to recover after we got home, and we were beyond grateful to be on the other side of that dramatic experience. It was such an intense ending to an otherwise memorable time together.

Malachi continued to have freak accidents happen to him over the course of the next year. He fell out of a window on the top floor of our friend's house in Seattle. He had an unexpected seizure in his crib at home one night that caused us to call an ambulance. It took us awhile to connect the Turkish woman's curse to that string of traumatic events.

One day, I was praying over my family and felt God highlight that moment in Turkey. Kate and I began to forcefully pray every night over our children and break off any curses, spells, decrees, or negative words spoken over them. We began to understand the power of spiritual warfare over the lives of our children.

We knew that it would be safer for us to stay home and raise our family in a safe suburban neighborhood in America. But we also knew God was calling us to pioneer a path of risk and adventure, following the voice of the Lord and not the echo of a convenient culture.

———

Our hearts began to expand exponentially for Muslims across the Middle East. We believed that we were stepping into a season that was prophesied. Even though our first experience ended with trauma, it was not enough to hold us back from pursuing what God had laid out for us.

In August 2014, I was on a plane bound for London, England, when I unexpectedly came face to face with God's passion for the Middle East. I was preparing to launch our new worship school in the English countryside where European leaders were gathering from across the continent. Directly following our school, we would join thousands in the fields of West Sussex for the third year of a seventy-two-hour nonstop worship festival called David's Tent. My mind was far from the Middle East.

I was fidgeting with my phone to get my last emails sent and messages downloaded before I ran out a of signal when I accidentally clicked on a link someone had sent to me. A video started playing that showed a man dressed in orange on his knees and another man dressed in black with a mask, holding a knife to the first man's neck. The landscape looked like somewhere in the desert. Before I could close the video, the man in black yelled something in Arabic and starting cutting into the neck of the man in orange. My plane took off and my phone froze on the video. I couldn't close it or stop it; it just kept playing until the very end.

The moment the video stopped, I was completely stunned and shocked. I could not believe what my eyes had seen. I could not unsee it. I had just accidentally watched the full video of the beheading of captured reporter James Foley. This happened at the hands of the ISIS leader Jihadi John, a British Muslim.

I did not know it at the time, but the video, leaked by the ISIS propaganda machine, went viral all over the world. The spirit of fear, intimidation, and torment spread like wildfire across the nations.

I could not sleep a wink the entire flight. My heart was completely enraged from that beheading video. I was angry that the peaceful people of the Middle East were threatened by a barbaric and satanic terrorist organization called ISIS. Not only that, but somehow Europe (and more specifically Britain) was exporting terrorists to the Middle East to wreak havoc on the ancient lands of biblical significance. This was a direct contradiction to their history and legacy. England has carried a rich revival history of sending worshipers and missionaries with hearts ablaze to spread the gospel of Jesus Christ to the corners of the earth.

A Davidic spirit rose up within me on the plane that night. What I can best describe as "righteous indignation" was welling up within me. Actually, it was boiling up within me and I could barely contain it sitting 35,000 feet in the air over the Atlantic.

As soon as the plane landed, we rushed to the worship school and I walked right in to speak at the first session. What is usually a happy and joyful message, welcoming people from around the world to our school, became something else entirely. The first altar call was for everyone to lay their lives down to bring the kingdom, love, and justice to the war zones across the world. I began the entire school where we normally would have ended it.

I felt like David when he showed up at the battlefield in time to witness the taunting spectacle of Goliath as he spewed out hatred and brought fear upon the people. In that moment, David spoke up and said, "Who is this uncircumcised Philistine that he should defy the armies of the living God?" (1 Samuel 17:26). That is exactly how I felt. Who could defy the armies of the living God? But first, we needed an army.

———

During that time, when ISIS was on the rise and taking control of large swaths of Iraq and Syria, fear was spreading across the US of an attack and an infiltration of terrorist activity. Many missionaries were leaving the region and Kurds, Yazidis, Christian Arabs, and other minority groups were being targeted and slaughtered.

I became frustrated with the lack of response to this crisis by American Christians at large. It seemed as though they responded more from fear than from faith. I really believed these were the exact moments we were born for. We do not raise up missionaries from fear, self-preservation, or caution. Jesus even commissioned the disciples as sheep among wolves (Matthew 10:16). The conferences and stadium events that were often the response of the Western Church were grinding at me. I felt like the Church was turning a blind eye to hundreds and even thousands being hunted down by ISIS and murdered each day.

This was the verse and the message that was burning in my soul.

> I hate, I despise your religious festivals;
> your assemblies are a stench to me.
> Even though you bring me burnt offerings and grain offerings,
> I will not accept them.
> Though you bring choice fellowship offerings,
> I will have no regard for them,
> Away with the noise of your songs!
> I will not listen to the music of your harps.
> But let justice roll on like a river,
> righteousness like a never-failing stream!
>
> Amos 5:21-24

During our mobilization efforts for the Middle East, I was leading worship at a conference at my home church in Harrisburg. Several of my friends leading other churches, movements, and organizations were in town that night, along with many mothers and fathers of the faith. It felt like a special moment with so many of us together under one roof. My pastor had an idea about doing a "passing of the baton" moment at the end of his message, based upon the verse in Psalm 145:4: "One generation commends your works to another."

Most of the young leaders were in their thirties, while the older generation of leaders were in their sixties. The moment felt holy. I could feel the
weight of God's presence as I walked with my friends onto the stage. One
of the spiritual leaders on the stage that day was Stacey Campbell, who
carries a strong prophetic gift. She has blessed us many times throughout
our lives and brought us incredible perspective, hope, and clarity. We had
enormous respect for her voice in our lives and in the Burn 24-7 movement.

At the end of the "passing of the baton" ceremony, the pastors, leaders, mothers, and fathers all prayed over us. Stacey came up and began to
prophesy over each person. Her words were powerful, hope-filled, and
encouraging—until she got to me. She spoke words of stadium evangelism,
mass media influence, stately apostolic leadership, and then she gave me
the word that I would despise for several years to come.

I stood at the end of the line where she had just given calm and loving
words of encouragement. When she got to me, she yelled out in a high-
pitched and authoritative voice:

"YOU, SEAN, ARE A MAN OF WAR! I SEE BLOOD
ALL OVER YOUR HANDS. YOU WERE MADE FOR
THE DAY OF BATTLE AND YOU WILL BE MISUN-
DERSTOOD BY MANY."

That was it. I couldn't believe it. There were no cheers, no loud "amens"
and everyone in the fifteen hundred seat auditorium sat awkwardly silent.

What happened? I thought. *No one wants to hear a word like that!* We
all want to be loved, championed, and understood. She had just spoken
a death decree. I hated every single word of that prophesy and tried my
hardest to forget it.

The word, however, would not let go of me.

CHAPTER 13

FINDING HOME

The following years in Pennsylvania were wild, invigorating, and somewhat chaotic. We pioneered multiple schools, started internships, released three albums, and had a third baby! This all happened while we traveled over 150,000 miles to at least a dozen nations each year. Kate and I were now outnumbered as a family of five. She fought hard against becoming the minivan soccer mom. She drove a Honda Pilot instead (which is basically the car of a minivan mom in denial).

At one point, we started feeling strained within our community. A few of our core leaders who had moved with us to Pennsylvania felt led to transition somewhere else. We were trying to juggle being present for all that was happening at home while also tending to the "fires" we had started across the world. It felt like we were torn in two at times, a feeling that meant neither side felt fully satisfied. There was also an element to our lives that most people in central Pennsylvania had a hard time understanding. I don't blame them; our lives were far from normal.

We wanted, for instance, to put our little girl in ballet classes on Wednesday night and then take her with us to Singapore and Indonesia for two weeks on Thursday morning. This was definitely not normal. The feeling of always trying to explain our heart, intentions, and motives to people started to wear on us. We were constantly apologizing to local friends because we felt led to leave for a month and visit our Burn communities in Europe, or South Africa, or South America. Our season no longer matched our community or the place we lived.

We tried for almost a year to ignore it. Through an absolute miracle, we had just purchased and restored the most gorgeous home of our entire lives. It was built in 1864 and was nestled on a hill next to a Civil War monument, overlooking the Susquehanna River. We had a beautiful and massive backyard where our kids would catch fireflies at night. It was our dream home, but we knew things were shifting.

———

During that same season, we landed a few brave and passionate souls to pioneer our ministry base in northern Iraq. They were all former babysitters at some point who had watched our kids—young, bright-eyed women who had never even been to the Middle East before. I have heard it said before that "God does not call the equipped, but He equips the called." Those courageous women were proof of that reality. Although they didn't meet the traditional qualifications of a missionary, they were the first ones to say yes.

With very little training, lots of prayer and fasting, and many difficult conversations with their family and friends, we sent them off into the middle of an active war zone in Iraq. ISIS was rearing its ugly head and the city of Mosul (ancient Nineveh) became the ISIS headquarters of operation. Our new Burn 24-7 base was established just forty miles down the road. While many organizations were bringing people home from the volatile region, we were sending three young, single American girls into the middle of it! You can only imagine the intense backlash, questioning, and judgments that were made about our organization.

A blanket of fear and paranoia covered the world because of that region. The Obama administration was doing very little to protect the defenseless and peaceful minority groups that had lived for hundreds of years in that area. ISIS was mercilessly slaughtering them. There was a new and horrendous atrocity highlighted almost every day in the news. Twitter feeds were rife with new beheading videos. The fear surrounding them was palpable.

One night when I was praying, I felt the Holy Spirit summon me into that crisis in a new way. I was not sure what more I could do as I traveled across America raising up willing hearts to lay down their lives for the people of Iraq. I was meditating on the story of Jonah and how he refused to follow his calling to bring the truth of God's word to the people of Nineveh. I vowed to never be the one who refused the leading of God to do something out of the box. As I made that vow, I instantly felt the call to take my family to Iraq on my next visit.

At first, I thought there was no way that was God. I assumed it was my own ambitions and good ideas. But then God started speaking to my wife about it as well. Ministering in the Middle East was still one of her greatest fears. My plan to have her fall in love with that region backfired when our baby boy got sick on our previous trip. I knew that if Kate had already come to the place of resolve and willingness to face that reality again, it could only be God!

We talked that night and she agreed that it was time to go and overcome those fears. I bought plane tickets right away for our family to go to Iraq the following month. It was a bold step of faith that many people disagreed with. I made the mistake of sharing about it on Facebook in order to help raise extra funds to bring the family along. People showed up to vocalize their opinions. The saddest part was that the negative remarks came primarily from Christians! My intentions were called into question and I was approached by many "well-meaning" people who tried to persuade me not to do something so foolish. The chorus of those voices grew so loud that for a moment I thought maybe I had not heard the Lord.

Due to the onslaught of opinions, Kate changed her mind and did not want to go anymore. Many others joined her plea to cancel the trip. But I dug my heels in. We were going to Iraq and I was bringing my wife and our three little kids. This was from God. I did not want our kids to grow up with a fear of the Middle East or a fear-based reaction toward Muslims or war zones like so many in America. All the media portrayed since the rise of ISIS was death and destruction that promoted fear toward that part of the world. I wanted my kids to see things from another perspective: God's perspective. I wanted them to witness firsthand God's power to transform places the world deemed were a lost cause.

Not only were my kids not clued into the fear-driven narrative of the Middle East, but they were genuinely excited to visit our team in Iraq (made up of their former babysitters) and all the beautiful refugees they were serving. Keturah asked me to make a lemonade stand that she could sit at every afternoon in our suburban Pennsylvania neighborhood. She wanted to raise money for toys to bring to the children who had recently escaped the grips of ISIS with only the shirts on their backs.

The next month, we landed in Istanbul with the entire family in tow. Our plane arrived late and we were pressed with urgency to make our connection to Erbil. It was a once-daily flight into Iraq and if we didn't make it, we would have to wait until the next day. We ran through the long airport terminals frantically searching for our gate, and finally arrived out of breath with crying and jet-lagged babies hanging from our hands. Those are the moments you do not post on Instagram for the world to see. There was nothing peaceful, aesthetic, or moving about that moment.

The gate was occupied with an entire room of Iraqis packed into the corner of the terminal, waiting to board. They looked at my blond-haired, blue-eyed babies all in tears and thought we must have the wrong departure gate. A sweet Arab lady approached us immediately to remind me that the gates for the flights to Europe were down the hall. I looked at her with a smile and assured her we were in the right place. The look on her face said it all! Another lady asked me over and over again why we would ever want to go to Iraq. She tried her hardest, through gestures and hand motions, to persuade us from our decision. We just smiled and waited for our turn to board.

That trip ended up being one of the most special experiences for my children. They still talk about it to this day. We arrived loaded with bags of goodies to give away to the refugees. Even Keturah's little pink backpack was full of pictures she had colored for the children. Not only was it a profound experience for our family, but we felt that it was also pivotal to show the world that God can meet you at the end of your fear if you simply become obedient to His voice.

We went to sleep every night hearing the rapid fire of machine guns. The apache helicopters buzzed right over our house. We were doing our best to help bring aid to the valiant Kurdish Peshmurga who were fighting ISIS on the front lines. All the while, my kids were unaware of the danger they were living in and actually never even asked. It was a massive lesson to me to become like a little child to inherit the kingdom God was bringing.

My own kids were the greatest agents of healing, kindness, and joy to the refugees. They showed up with smiles, toys, candy, and the occasional jet-lagged meltdown as well. But they thrived in that environment and Kate and I went to sleep every night astonished at the light they carried with them into the war zone. It was a testimony of God's grace.

Our second day on the ground, the vision that Kate had in the bathtub in Dallas years before suddenly became a reality. As we walked hand in hand with our kids in a refugee camp, Kate suddenly stopped and burst into tears. She turned to me and said, "It's happening! The moment God showed me years ago when I saw this and heard a voice ask me, 'Will you trust Me with your children?'"

After wrestling with the decision to bring our kids into an active war zone and the blowback from people telling us how foolish we were, God met us. We were standing in her vision of white tents and our children beside us in the Middle East—a vision that had taken place while we battled infertility, before we even had any children of our own.

Every parent has to come to a moment of fully releasing their child to Jesus—trusting Him that He can take care of them better than we ever could. We were there, right in the middle of that moment. We could feel God's presence and His pleasure all around us.

———

When we returned home, it became even more clear in our hearts that it was time for our family to transition into a new season. We felt unsettled and we believed we had accomplished what God had sent us to Harrisburg to do. A season that began with the loss of my own father ended with me learning how to become a father to my own children and discovering the legacy I wanted to leave behind for them. I was so grateful for our family and friends there and for the many spiritual fathers that stepped into our lives in that season, but I had no idea where God was calling us to or, really, why we were going.

That spring, I flew out to Redding, California, for a songwriting trip with other worship leaders. I had many friends there and had been invited as a guest to conferences, worship schools, and gatherings many times before. Bethel Church and everyone in that community felt like family to us. In the past, different leaders had invited us to move out there, but we never felt it was right. It was always about 115 degrees when we visited in the dead of summer, and I was definitely not a hot-weather person. I was also resistant to joining spiritually known "hot spots" of the world. In reality, I often preached against it! I would encourage young leaders to pioneer and search for cities, regions, and communities where there was *not* a church or ministry on every corner. I encouraged people to birth something new.

Yet, God did something deep in me during that writing trip. Not only did I feel heaven open up over our time together as we wrote some incredible songs, but my heart was connecting in a different way to the community. Doing life together with my friends for just a week made such an impact on my heart and I could feel my creativity ignited for music and songwriting.

I returned from that trip and, half-jokingly, asked my wife if we should move to Redding. She just laughed at me. She knew how much I loved pioneering and did not want to join an already crowded movement. She also reminded me of how I had told people in the past not to move to Redding because they probably would never leave! She thought it was ironic that I would even joke about it.

We talked about it for minute together. In jest, she said, "Just keep your phone on, because someone will probably send you a dream if God is on it at all." The next morning I woke up to a text message from a friend of mine. He had a dream about our family where we were standing in Bill Johnson's backyard. Bill is the Senior Leader at Bethel Church. The whole sequence was so absurdly synchronized with our conversation the night before that it could only be God.

A few other confirmations followed that event, but I was still somewhat reluctant to move to California. I had only returned from my writing trip less than a month before, so we decided to send Kate on a scouting trip to look at the area, scope out potential homes, and visit the local schools. She quickly fell in love with the area. I tried to remind her that it was likely because it was spring and not a thousand degrees. Besides, everything was green and lush at that time of year in Northern California.

Just like with our transition out of Dallas, I put the same fleece before the Lord about our house in Pennsylvania. We had moved into our beautiful and historic dream home less than two years prior. We had also dumped quite a bit of money into fixing it up—it really felt magazine and Pinterest worthy! I was warned it would take years to get that money back. But I went ahead and put a "For Sale By Owner" sign in the yard.

That same day, someone called us with a full-price cash offer. My real estate friends were shocked. I knew exactly what it meant, however. God had made it abundantly clear we were called to follow His voice to California.

CHAPTER 14

POLITICAL CALLING

Our first few months in Redding were very hot but very fruitful. It felt like we could breathe again. We felt acceptance to show up and be ourselves without the pressure of expectations. I didn't realize how badly we needed that until we actually got there. It was the first time in our marriage where we did not have to plant and pioneer an element of the community but could simply join an already thriving one. It was also a place where we really felt understood.

We had many authentic friendships in our former communities with people who are our close friends to this day. But in Redding, we were no longer the odd ones out. There are a lot of big personalities and global ministries based in Redding. It is a place of high ceilings and tall windows.

It is a community that can tolerate and even celebrate taking your children to a war zone on spring break. While that probably wasn't the norm, it still felt much less weird than in other places we'd lived.

Our new home and community shared the mindset that you can do anything God has set before you, and we were grateful. We felt covered, championed, and looked after. I accepted an invitation to join the Bethel Music label in leading worship and songwriting. I felt God's hand on the creativity in my heart. Kate began to make friends. My kids fell in love with their new school. We were loving our new property and community.

About a year after we moved to Redding, my family was flourishing in a new and special way. We felt like we were finally home.

———

In the midst of joining a thriving and well-known record label, receiving invitations to some of the biggest and well-known worship events in the world, and adding to our family—we had our fourth child—something else was stirring in my heart and keeping me up at night. I could not shake the thought of the sticky note stuck to my old bedroom wall. I had, at that point, visited three of the five nations on that list: Afghanistan, North Korea, and Iraq. Considering how closed, isolated, and dangerous many of those nations are, I thought I had done well for myself.

I had pretty much given up, however, on the last two countries. There were seasons when I felt compelled to look into connections, opportunities, or any way to visit those countries. I exhausted every single resource I had. Many years, many relationships, and many hours of research didn't open a single door.

We had been in Redding a few years when the Holy Spirit began to remind me about the unfinished work and provoked my heart to dream again. I fought it off for a few months and tried to silence the voice—after all, wasn't I running enough initiatives already?

Finally, with a one-month gap between two international trips, I decided to use it as a window to send in my passport for a visa. It was not just any visa, but one of the hardest in the world to get. My goal was to secure a five-year multiple-entry visa into the Kingdom of Saudi Arabia. It was not just one of the most difficult visas to obtain, but you need a very convincing reason to get it. The paperwork alone was excruciating. The State Department also advised Americans against traveling to the region.

The tensions between Sunnis and Shias was reaching a new boiling point across the region. Saudi Arabia is known to punish, imprison, and kill nationals who convert from Islam to Christianity. They have a long history of persecuting the Church both inside and outside of the country. In addition to the atrocities committed against Christians inside their borders, they have radicals planted in many different neighboring nations that incite violence against Christian minority groups.

I filled out the long application including dates, details, and more. There was one important question on the top of the application that I did not know how to answer: "Purpose of Visit." After praying for a few days, wanting to make sure that I was honest on the application, I filled in the blank with "Official Kingdom Business." I was almost certain my application would be rejected, and if not, there would definitely be follow-up questions.

After sending in the passport, it was just a matter of waiting for a response. After two weeks without a reply, I began to call the embassy. Each day I called, and each day someone would pick up the phone yelling in Arabic and then hang up. This same thing happened for a week. I even had one of my friends in Washington, DC drive over to the embassy to check on the visa. Still, we didn't hear anything. Finally, after three weeks of waiting, I began to get nervous. My next international trip was coming up and I needed my passport back. I called the embassy again and just asked them to send my passport back without the visa. I told them I would pay overnight shipping charges.

A few days later, my dog ran up to me on my porch with a post office envelope hanging out of his mouth. Half of the envelope was torn off and there was no return address listed. That was the first time my dog had ever done anything like that! I looked into the ripped side of the envelope and saw my passport inside with no other documents attached. I was immediately relieved but also incredibly bewildered. Where did it come from and how did it even get here? I opened the passport and began to thumb through the seventy pages of stamps and visa stickers. Near the back of the booklet, I saw an unfamiliar entry and caught my breath. It was a five-year multiple-entry visa to Saudi Arabia! The reason for my visit was stamped across the visa: OFFICIAL KINGDOM BUSINESS!

———

The moment my feet hit the ground in Riyadh, the capitol of Saudi Arabia, I could feel a sense of safety, peace, and authority from God. I knew it was the culmination of the endless hours of prayers I prayed since returning from that first mission trip to Brazil.

Just prior to my trip, I happened to get connected with a local pastor. He invited me to lead worship at an underground worship gathering, part of a collaboration of churches. It was secretive and mobilized through an intricate and secure messaging application. The message was to meet at a specific location in the desert and "to bring a fire in your heart to worship Jesus." The details were purposefully vague but enough to guide people in the right direction. The Saudi pastors were pros at orchestrating gatherings for a very isolated, scattered, and persecuted Church.

Most of my closest friends understand that I would rather lead worship in a room of ten underground church leaders than in a public stadium of ten thousand. In fact, most of the moments that have marked my life in worship have not happened in America. They have occurred all over the world in the most unlikely places and situations.

The boldness and courage demonstrated by the Church in Saudi Arabia, along with the risks associated with simply gathering in worship together, certainly presented an unlikely situation. Their sacrifice was a magnet attracting the nearness of God! Those will be the heroes in heaven one day. They will be the names or ministries we never knew on the earth, but they were known in heaven.

As we pulled up to the hidden location that night, I could immediately hear the rumble of voices inside. I was completely shocked—I had imagined this being a small gathering of leaders, hidden away in someone's home. Instead, I walked into a crowd of 1,200 to1,500 of the most passionate worshipers I had ever seen in my entire life. They had no band, no fog machine, no production or mood lighting. It was just raw and unbridled adoration for Jesus as they cried out for more! One of the pastors turned to me with a smile and said, "They have been here for over two hours like this waiting for you to come lead them in worship."

I immediately broke down in tears and crumpled to the floor. The raw passion, hunger for Jesus, and sacrifice of praise mingled together and rose up like an offering before the Lord. What took place over the next few hours was nothing short of heavenly. I had no desire to lead worship; I wanted to be led by *them* to the secret places of God's heart. I stayed mostly on the floor, getting up to sing at certain points randomly throughout the night. Wave after wave of spontaneous emotional expression to Jesus crashed over us—weeping, laughter, joy, and the profound reality of God's nearness and love. Then I realized that this gathering was normal. This was not just an expression of excitement for a one-time event. These worshipers were stewarding this fire in their homes and secret locations all over the nation. The intense fear and persecution they face daily for following Jesus created a sound inside of them that cannot be muted. Their worship could not be silenced.

After returning home from the trip, my priorities, aspirations, and even some dreams began to shift in my heart. We were actively engaged with long-term teams and projects around the Middle East, but my heart wanted so much more. I was praying and fasting to see if what God was doing inside of me was the beginning of another massive transition. Even though things were going great with my family, our home, our prayer and mission organizations, and the music label, there was a new level of risk God was calling us to. I just had no idea what it was.

I wanted to live on the edge again with God. I felt very safe in that season, and being with the Saudi underground church reminded me of how I was called to live—with brazen faith. I know I was born for risk and adventure with God. The older we grow and the more "established" we become in our families, finances, businesses, and ministries, the harder it is to leave the comfort of what we've built. This is why I believe Jesus said, "It is easier for a camel to go through the eye of a needle than for someone who is rich to enter the kingdom of God" (Matthew 19:24). When we have so much to lose, we do not want to lose anything.

There was a deep groaning in my heart to be back to that place of dependency on God, and I could not shake it. I told Kate that maybe we should just sell everything and move to Iraq with our long-term missions team. I was actually serious and looked into some options, timelines, and ways to make that happen.

A few months later, while we were preparing for our annual Bethel Music conference in Los Angeles, another random idea came to my mind. The only reason I paid attention to it was because it seemed so absurd and different than anything I had ever thought or dreamed of before. I leaned over to Kate one night before going to sleep and jokingly said, "Maybe I missed my calling and was supposed to somehow engage in politics."

I had always carried a passion for this arena and knew how much it affected every single person's life on the planet— especially American politics. The beginning of every year, I made it a point to have a watch party for the president's State of the Union speech. Regardless of who was president throughout the years of my life, I always made a plan to watch and analyze the speech.

I wasn't always in love with America. I wanted to leave right after high school, especially as I felt the spiritual fabric of the nation eroding. The increasing secularization of the Church and the spiritual apathy were overwhelming. I was skeptical that things would ever change.

After traveling to over sixty nations around the world, however, and understanding the cultural, political, economic, and social paradigms of so many other places, I began to have a greater sense of patriotism. I also saw the enormous influence that American politics has all over the world. Despite the criticism and pain that come with being the "world's policeman," there also comes an incredible opportunity to promote freedom, justice, and the gospel message that was inherent in the founding of America.

When I said that to my wife that night, she looked at me and smiled, saying, "You'd probably make a good politician because you'd stand up for what's right and don't care what people think." Then we both went to sleep and didn't think about it again.

———

The opening night of the conference in downtown Los Angeles, I was feeling restless and had been all day. I knew the gathering was going to be amazing, but I had lost excitement for it and all other events like it. I usually love these gatherings because our entire Bethel Music family gathers from across America and it's the one time of year we get to see everyone. Yet, I had zero energy and zeal for it this time around.

Then a moment happened in the green room that night that changed the game for us. We are still living in the fruit of that "suddenly." As we were getting ready to pray as a team that night, several pastors, leaders, musicians, and guests were in the room. One of them, whom I had never met before, walked up to me. He was a very tall, older, well-dressed gentleman whom I had seen earlier with the leaders of my church.

He approached me and said, "Your name is Sean, right?"

I said, "Yeah."

"Man, I've been following you for a while," he continued, "and love how you navigate life, family, and politics."

"Thanks so much, but what do you mean politics?" I said.

"Well, I really believe you are going to run for US Congress," he replied. "It is all over you, man. We need a long-haired, Jesus-loving worship leader in there. It's time for you to be a voice for a generation. It's time for a change. You *are* that change."

Before I could even grasp everything he said, the moment was interrupted by a call to gather for corporate prayer. I was completely shocked. *What was it that he just said? I was going to run in politics?* I had zero desire to enter into politics at the time and that conversation a few nights earlier had been a half-hearted joke. Even though I did not acknowledge it in the moment, those words he spoke in that room, while standing around some of my spiritual heroes, ate away at me. I tossed and turned that night in bed and could not sleep.

The next morning, during the conference, I was getting ready to lead worship when I bumped into that same man. Before addressing the previous night's bizarre prophecy, I asked him who he was. He mentioned that he was a businessman, investor, and had helped run Pat Robertson's presidential campaign back in the 1980s. He talked about how he witnessed a wave of believers from every age, race, and background engage in the political realm after they saw such a notable Christian figure like Pat run for president. "It was like it gave Christians across America permission," he said. "From that moment forward, believers began to run for everything from governor to dog catcher in elections. Many of them won and are still in politics today from that era."

This conversation only served to stir my heart even more and complicate my already complicated life with a myriad of questions, desires, longings, and even missed opportunities. It awakened something inside of me and I could not turn it off.

When the conference was over and we drove home, I could not stop thinking about that man's words. Over the past few years, in the midst of our busy lives of ministry, we had received hundreds if not thousands of words from different communities and individuals. Some of them have been so far out there that they could only be made up in someone's imagination or directly from the Spirit of God. This word belonged in that same category.

The gentleman had given me his number and we communicated over the next few weeks. He wanted me to take the next steps and really explore the possibility of getting involved in politics. He said he had helped many past candidates and reiterated again and again that I had what it takes to run a successful campaign and win a seat in Congress.

After many phone calls back and forth, including conference calls with a team of advisors and consultants that he connected me to in Washington, DC, I decided I could no longer push this aside. I needed to at least go visit everyone in DC and rule out the potential for running. Not only did I not know if I had it in my heart to run, but I would be in a massive time-crunch since the primary was fast approaching. I would need to invest in some insane fundraising efforts, not to mention find a close district that was winnable in California to run in.

On my flight to DC, I researched the name and background of the team that I was going to visit. They were referred to me by Michael Clifford, who gave me the prophetic word in the green room in Los Angeles. They were widely esteemed in the political circles and I could not even believe they would give me the time of day! Not once did they toot their own horn on their accomplishments, but man, oh man, every single person on the team had some serious experience! They ran several incredibly successful congressional and senate races in the past twenty years, and they also ran point on Dr. Ben Carson's presidential campaign in 2016.

Dr. Carson's was the campaign I had followed most closely and it had given me hope for politics! I loved that he was a Christian and a brain surgeon—the first to successfully separate conjoined twins in the late 1980s. He was not particularly charismatic, yet he was transformed into a very popular, likable, and almost winning candidate for the Republican Party. He seemed to break the mold of the old, stiff white guy that dominated conservatism—and politics in general—for so long. I loved that he was bold in his witness for Jesus, as well. I always wondered about the team behind him and marveled at their ability to create such a clean, positive, and powerful campaign that much of America (and the church) rallied behind.

There I was, on my way to Washington, DC, invited by that very same team. It was actually unfathomable, at the time, that God had set me up like that! The knowledge of who I was visiting increased my expectations for that trip.

We spent three jam-packed, glorious days together running all over the district. We met with senators, congressmen, and advisors, and spent hours looking at a potential 2020 race from every single angle. We visited the Republican National Committee headquarters and discussed funding and what I would need to raise to win this race. They told me, with a smile, that running in Northern California would be a "cheaper race" and that I would only need to raise two to three million to be competitive. I took a deep breath. Although I had taken many risks to raise millions for refugees in the previous years, political causes seemed much more daunting. I did not even know how it would be possible to raise so much, and I could not wrap my mind around that kind of money.

We sat for hours together and they answered every single question I had. I was praying under my breath the entire time and really trying to make sure I was hearing God. I wanted to remain in a mindset of being as "wise as serpents and harmless as doves" (Matthew 10:16). I was warned by many people that I would be manipulated or controlled by consultants in Washington. I was told they were only interested in seeing how much money I could raise so they could take a cut.

I never felt that once from that group of consultants. In fact, after we had spent that much time together—weighing the overall cost to my family, career, and current projects—they still told me not to feel any pressure. As I was leaving their office to catch my plane back to California, they turned to me and said, "You should let your wife make the final decision. She needs to know what you are stepping into. Whatever she says, goes." That was the moment when I knew I could trust them.

That entire flight home, my heart came alive and was pounding with nervous energy. I somehow knew everything in my life was going to radically change. I was not exactly sure what it would look like and I was not fully convinced that I was even going to accept their backing and run for Congress in 2020. But I was feeling something I had not felt in a long, long time: I was in way over my head.

———

I wasn't sure if Kate would really want me to dive into politics. After all my interviews and time spent assessing the overall cost and toll on the family, it really did not feel practical at all. I was also not looking for more stuff to do. I didn't need a career change. I was happily married with four amazing kids—Keturah, Malachi, Ezra, and Zion—and we were running three successful non-profits to support global missions, the Burn movement, and child sponsorship. I was traveling over 200,000 miles every year, and writing and recording with one of the biggest worship music labels in the world. My life was hitting on all cylinders.

It was the risk, danger, and the unknown, however, that were calling out to me. It was like an invitation that was hard to refuse. So many times

I wish that I had not been created with this affection for such a risk-filled life. It would make things much easier for me and my family if I could just settle down and be satisfied with the status quo. At thirty-six years old, we had already accomplished so much (or at least, that is what my wife kept telling me). But I can rarely ever seem to dwell on that. All I can think about is what is over the next mountain, probably to a fault. I just can't seem to help it. Either I find the place of risk or the risk seems to find me. I am still not quite sure how it all works.

I was convinced my wife would not be on board with the plan to run for Congress. With the possibility of living bi-locationally between DC and California, I knew it would be a tough sell for her. She was pretty settled into our routine in Redding and was really in love with the pace and season we were in. After years of moving all over America, having four kids, and my insane travel schedule, she deserved it. The very least I could do was create some measure of consistency for her to live in. She is much more of a homebody than I am and I felt like I had put her through a lot. It seemed very selfish to chase another wild idea at this point in my life.

The moment I arrived home from DC and walked into the house, Kate looked at me and said, "Uh oh, you have the look in your eye again, babe. I know what that means." I kept prodding her to explain what she meant, what she saw after looking at me for only a split second. "You have a light in your eyes," she said. "It is something that I have not seen in a while. I have missed that."

That was before I told her all the hard things, like how tough it would actually be if we chose this option in life right now. I tried to explain how many friends we would lose, how much money we would have to raise, and then the sheer traveling nightmare it would create if I did actually win. We agreed to pray and fast for a few days and then make a final decision.

I had a full travel schedule lined up the following week, plus countless meetings, projects, deadlines, and things in my orbit at home. With a decision looming over me, everything felt much more difficult to accomplish.

It weighed heavy on my mind at all times. I was counting the cost over and over again. I went back and forth with options in my mind to see and feel if it was really all worth it. It is one thing to be a musician, a missionary, and a guy who helps refugees in Iraq and children at risk in India. But the moment you lift up your hand to become a politician—and in California, of all places—your entire world becomes polarized.

I continued to remind myself that being in politics was never my dream. I never aspired to be a politician. So why would I lay down all I had built and established to chase something that had never been in my heart before? The answer became simple and more defined as the days wore on.

As I pondered my decision, I began to look at my children in a different light. All the prayers I had prayed as a teenager standing on the National Mall in DC came rushing back to me. I remember repeating a prayer with the other 400,000 gathered believers that God would raise up leaders in America who would stand for justice and righteousness. We prayed that the death decree of abortion established by Roe vs. Wade in 1973 would be broken. Now I found myself faced with a challenge: was I willing to personally become a fulfillment of those prayers?

About three days into our fasting and prayer time, I walked into our room where Kate sat, holding her phone in her hand. She stared at me. She had read one of the new crazy bills that were about to pass in California. A child, who cannot even get their ears pierced at fifteen years old without their parents' permission, would now be approved, funded, and secretly hidden by the state for a sex change as young as the age of twelve. I have rarely seen my wife as livid as she was in that moment. She looked at me and said, "Babe, you're doing this. It has to happen now. It is getting so crazy and someone has to do something!"

I had never seen her so certain of anything in my life. Ironically, I was now the one riddled with uncertainty and anxiety. She was totally convinced. When Kate gets her mind on something, she's unmovable. I was feeling far from unmovable. Even after all the crazy confirmations, miracles, and open doors, I began to think of the trajectory of my life and calling. I had worked so hard for so many years with diligence and persistence in music and ministry. I was approaching what many may call the "precipice" of my career in terms of notoriety and influence.

I had finally learned to successfully balance my non-profits, travel, recording, and even some side businesses to keep everything going. Was I really willing to completely derail all of the ease and even "grace" of that to step into something unknown and potentially career ending? Was I willing to trade being liked and accepted for potentially being despised and misunderstood?

When you are known for helping people around the world and you sing songs for a living, there is a general consensus that you are a good guy. We had experienced a fair amount of resistance over the years, but I knew it was nowhere near what we would face in the political arena. It was an invitation into hardship and resistance. The level of warfare (seen and unseen) was tangible. We had already received many warning calls from friends, leaders, and advisors reminding us that the political realm was not a place to walk into lightly. I even had someone write and circulate a letter explaining all of the reasons why I was not equipped to do this. Was I really willing to face this resistance for a race that I was told would not even be winnable?

At this point in my journey, my original idea of moving to Iraq with my family seemed like a far easier decision! A seed of doubt had taken root in my mind. Was I really ready to give up everything to step into this promise? What would it mean for the future of my family? What would it mean for the future of my non-profits, my career?

Despite all these thoughts, my wife was 100 percent convinced that I should run. Through it all, something that I could not get off my mind was the "Man of War" word from Harrisburg years earlier. I can't even explain how much I absolutely hated that word; yet, it was eating away at me. Was this my "Man of War" moment?

CHAPTER 15

MOMENTUM

I declared my campaign for Congress in the beginning of August 2019. We had to set our face like flint to go for an all-out sprint until the March primaries in 2020. During my trip to DC, the team of advisors and I had scoured the map of Northern California to find a vulnerable district with need of a fresh change and a new face. In the state of California, a candidate running for Congress does not have to live within the district they represent. This occurs more than you would think as the boundary lines between districts change after every census. Members of Congress have ended up residing in a district other than the one they represent because the lines are continually redrawn.

The district where I lived was historically conservative with good congressional representation already in place. But there was a particular district that straddled the city of Sacramento and the Bay Area, with large swaths of farmland in between. It was the most ethnically diverse district in the state. It also contained one of the highest concentrations of millennials of any district in California. Everything on paper looked promising to run in district three.

It was eye-opening to see how much detailed information you can find on voters in a particular district. Not only can you tell what party each individual voted for in the past ten elections, but you can analyze their media consumption, eating habits, and even their travel habits. This was all such new territory for me and pulled back the veil on how the political system functions.

The consultants in DC were also convinced that 2020 was the right race for me because of who I would be going up against. The sitting congressman was a forty-five-year career politician who did not have a great reputation in the community and was not winning by a large margin each election cycle. He was very far left wing in most of his votes on the floor, yet he represented a very "purple" and diverse constituency. He had served under the Clinton administration, the State Assembly in California, as Lieutenant Governor, and was currently district three's representation in the US Congress.

It seemed like it was being set up rather nicely. My consultants, advisors, and friends started to slowly win me over to their excitement and the sheer challenge of taking on a long-time political giant. The dichotomy was unmistakable. It was David versus Goliath. He had it all—power, money, resources, and the backing of every major Democratic ally (including the Clintons, Obamas, and the current governor of California). I was the political outsider with hardly any money, zero political experience, and no strong endorsements. I was a young, long-haired millennial worship leader going up against a seventy-four-year-old professional politician. Who had ever heard of something so absurd in the political world?

I thought that maybe this would ignite a fire in a generation of millennials who have been disengaged from politics. What if something about this God storyline would awaken the Church to become the salt and the light again in Washington, DC? Was there any way to bring redemption to the often perceived darkness in politics?

So much of the political world is based on first-time impressions. It is actually very shallow in many ways. Our hope was that we would get noticed by the press because our story was so unique. After all, I was running in the liberal state of California! Much of America had written our state off as the farthest corner of liberalism (nearing socialism).

Some of the most horrendous and anti-Christ legislation imaginable was being created and then pumped out of the capital city of Sacramento. It was becoming the prototype of governmental control: state-funded abortions, high taxes, excessive crime, mandatory vaccines, and attacks against religious liberty. There was not much good news coming out of our state. With the raging wildfires, power outages, and exploding homeless population, residents were fleeing by the thousands every day, and it appeared that the state would lose an entire congressional seat due to population decline alone! This was something that had never happened in history.

Known commonly as the "left coast" and sometimes mocked by other states and leaders, those outside California do not always know of the gold that still lies within the "Golden State." Some of the most significant revivals in the last hundred years took place in California. Azusa Street in the early 1900s and the Jesus People Movement in the 1960s and 1970s brought a wave of salvation, healing, and hope to the nation! If God did it once in this state, why not again?

Anytime I travel, I try to explain clearly that there is another "California" inside of California that many people do not know about. They are family people. They are people of faith. They stand up for parental rights when it comes to education, medicine, and overregulation. They have a strong moral center and their voices are not being represented in government.

My optimistic personality thought: Why can't we change the narrative? What if we could take a stand in a place everyone else thought was hopeless and raise our voice? What if the Church became engaged unlike any time in history to actually vote their value and stand up? The statistics reveal in California alone that only half of all Christians are registered to vote. Only half of those registered will actually vote in a presidential election year. It is far less than that in a non-presidential cycle.

What if we could break down the political barriers and I could somehow represent the majority of Americans who live in the center of the two extremes? What if we were not so polarized? Maybe I could be the candidate to bring people together in our state. Ronald Reagan is a prime example of how successful California can be when it is united together. Why couldn't it happen again several decades later? At this point, I was completely naive, or maybe God just tricked me into the whole thing.

———

We soon found out that there were two other contenders running in the district three congressional race. They had already been running for many months and had quite a head start on me. I needed to formulate a concrete plan, do some initial fundraising, and make a big splash to announce my campaign. It would also become a game of catch-up all the way until the March primary. Once I made my commitment, though, there could be no turning back. I had to be all in!

We officially launched the campaign on September 27, 2019, in a historic park in Vacaville, California, which was the population epicenter of the district. I wanted it to look and feel different from a typical campaign launch. It had to be something fresh and genuinely me. I didn't want it to even be political (as crazy as that sounds). I wanted my launch to represent the celebration of something new and exciting. So we went with the "Jesus

People Movement" bohemian vibe and we took the party outside.

We hired a large sound system and gathered hundreds of people from across the region for worship, prayer, and my first speech as a candidate for Congress. We live-streamed the entire thing on Facebook, Instagram, and YouTube and flung it far and wide across the internet. Thousands were tuning in and engaging who probably had never paid attention to a political campaign in their lives! My four kids came dressed up in USA gear, dancing across the stage to a song we wrote together called "Raise Our Voice." The atmosphere was bright, electric, and so full of joy. It was the most unique political function I had ever been part of and gave me great hope for the campaign.

My Twitter feed blew up and my Instagram campaign video was viewed and shared more than anything I had ever posted before. During the recap call with my campaign team in DC the next day, they remarked how they had never seen that amount of engagement for a congressional launch before. They reviewed the analytics and buzz on social media and touted how it far eclipsed even presidential candidates they had represented. This was such a massive boost of hope to my heart; I had no frame of reference for what was even normal. I was as surprised as anyone else that there was wind blowing on this new venture.

Major media outlets covered our launch day, and I even had an interview with Fox News as our campaign website and video gained considerable traction. It was no longer just California news, either. My campaign became a national and even an international story. Outlets as far away as London, England, and Johannesburg, South Africa, were now following and writing about the campaign. It seemed like many in the church were energized and the prayers and donations of many people I had never met were pouring in! Our website was inundated with media requests. It seemed like everything was going in the right direction and our prophetic words were coming to pass.

———

In December, I received an invitation to join a diverse group of young faith leaders for a briefing at the White House. The focus and topic was religious liberty. We streamed in from across the nation to hear the policies and goals of the administration around this topic.

I've always dreamed about receiving an invitation to the White House. I never really cared who the president was or what his policies were; I just always wanted to see God move in a place as powerful, historic, and monumental as the White House. I would have gone (and still will go) to visit any president or prime minster, regardless of their reputation or political stance. Government is a God-ordained door that believers are called to walk through without fear of retribution from today's "cancel culture." Everyone from Moses, Daniel, David, and Jesus to Billy Graham and Martin Luther King, Jr. stepped through this door to pray, share, and bring God's presence to the kings of the earth. I felt so honored to be even just a fly on the wall in the room that day!

One of the words I have carried my entire life comes from Isaiah 22:22, to step into open doors that no man can shut and shut doors that no man can open. That meeting at the White House was one of those moments. It was a reoccurring gathering of pastors and leaders that began one year earlier. Due to unforeseen circumstances (which are changing daily at the White House), no senior officials were present or engaged with the group during the first year. For some reason, I felt this year would be different, and I booked my tickets to Washington, DC.

When we gathered at the corner of the White House complex to enter through Secret Service, I felt the Holy Spirit tell me to wait until the last person in line to enter. So I hung around the corner while the other sixty leaders entered the security protocol. All of a sudden a black SUV pulled up to the corner and out stepped Newt Gingrich, the former speaker of the

House! He was running late to a White House Christmas party and was carrying a bag full of gifts in his hand. I approached him and shared who I was and what I was doing in California. His face lit up with excitement as he spoke loudly to me, "You are exactly what California and America need right now!" We took a few pictures together and I even had him share his three-point strategy on how he would solve the homelessness and housing crisis we were facing in my state. I was dumbfounded and elated! I thought maybe that moment was the entire reason that I came.

I finally went through security and entered into the Eisenhower building where we were gathering to begin our day with worship. As I was scoping the room, I turned and saw Vice President Mike Pence walk in. I knew several people who know him personally and they had always exclaimed what a deep man of faith he was. I looked up to him for his bold stance on America returning to the values of faith, family, and prayer. I happened to be standing next to him and his security detail the moment he came into the room. I leaned over to him during the worship and introduced myself. He was kind and almost had a childlike glee as he told me, "I heard there was worship going on here today and I had to cancel everything I was doing to come and be part of this! This is the most important thing happening in this building today!"

It was not a tame worship service, either. It was passionate, fiery, and full of emotion as the leaders sang their hearts out. We were part of one of the most diverse groups of leaders that could have assembled. We were racially, denominationally, and theologically diverse. We represented many different movements across America and I was honored to be in that room.

A few songs into the meeting, I shared with the vice president that I was a worship leader and also running for Congress in California. His expression was unforgettable as he smiled and said, "Wow! This is exactly what Congress needs right now! A worshiper going to Capitol Hill. I love it!" Before he left the room, he turned to me and said,

"I will be watching your race, Sean!"

Wild! I just got a personal shout-out from the vice president of the United States of America!

One by one, senior White House officials addressed our group, including former Governor Sam Brownback (ambassador at large for International Religious Freedom) and Ivanka Trump (senior advisor to the president). Every single official was grateful that we would gather in the White House to worship, pray, and engage in their decision-making policy on various governmental issues.

Toward the end of the day, an announcement was made that we were to immediately walk toward the West Wing and that the president himself wanted to personally address our group! We were all floored. This was divinely historic.

As we hurried along with security to the West Wing, I overheard one of the White House aides tell her friend, "I can't believe Trump is doing this today! It's the middle of the impeachment and he's cancelled so much!" Apparently, the president had been pretty shut off to visitors while he navigated the House of Representatives' move to impeach him. This was only the third time in US history this had happened to a sitting president.

When we arrived at the West Wing, we entered yet another security clearance. They took all our cellphones and we stepped into the historic cabinet room. At the center of the room was a giant wooden table surrounded by old leather chairs where the president meets with his cabinet members each week. There was a fireplace in the middle of the room with busts of George Washington and Benjamin Franklin at one end and a painting of Alexander Hamilton at the other. The decisions made in this room affected virtually every facet of life in America.

As we were taking in our surroundings, the door swung open and President Trump stepped into the room. We were all stunned to see him there, in the same room as us. He kindly but firmly addressed our group and then asked us to pray for him and his administration. He told us that they needed our prayers in this time like no other.

Right as we were about to pray, he looked at us and then gestured to his security detail. "Hey! Why don't we do this inside the Oval Office?" he said. "What do you guys think about that?" Of course we cheered, and seconds later we were shuffled into the historic Oval Office through a trap door in the wall. Inside, I was genuinely FREAKING OUT! I think we all were in that moment, while trying our hardest to play it cool.

Trump mentioned that he had an important phone call with China but wanted to show us the Oval Office and have us pray over him while he sat at the Resolute desk. As soon as he sat down, we laid hands on him and prayed the most passionate and fiery prayers. He closed his eyes, smiled, and nodded as we went for it. Upon finishing the last prayer, I hung around toward the back in hopes I could personally greet him before we left. He told us, "You guys are great, but I gotta get on this phone call with China!"

I extended my hand to him, he shook it politely, and then I leaned into him, saying, "My name is Sean Feucht and I am a worship leader running for Congress in California's third district." He smiled at me and said, "That is amazing! Good luck! I will be watching your race now!"

Just a few months into announcing my campaign and I had the president of the United States comment that he was going to watch my race! I was the last one to leave the Oval Office that day.

The official White House pictures that came out of our visit to the Oval Office spread like wildfire around the world—or at least the Twitter universe! We became the target for drama in church circles, as well. The number of people who hated that we went to pray in that room was astounding! Who knew that sixty worship leaders and pastors crammed into the most important room in the world would cause such a ruckus?

That picture and story attracted such an immense amount of backlash for everyone in that room. We chose to celebrate the moment anyway. It felt like God had supernaturally called us to carry His presence into the highest office of the land!

I believed our prayers and worship were going to change something. Similar to my trips to Uganda, North Korea, Iraq, Saudi Arabia, and Afghanistan, I believe heaven responds with power in moments of risk and sacrifice. I came home from that trip with more confidence and faith than ever that God was going to shock the political world through my congressional race.

CHAPTER 16

DEFEAT

I hit the ground running and devoted all my time and attention to California's district three. I went to every meeting, political gathering, and church service that I could find in order to share my perspective on why our state was in crisis and needed change. Every single day I was stepping into open doors with senators, congressmen, and top leaders around the world. God was really moving and breathing on my campaign in a phenomenal way.

Politics is such a strange business. It demands that candidates become the biggest self-promoters, as you are really selling yourself in a way. It also forces conversations on a myriad of issues where you often have to come up with divine (or sometimes crazy) solutions on the spot. I prayed continually, asking for divine wisdom. I did not physically have the time nor space to research all of the topics that came up on the campaign trail. There were agriculture and water issues, tax issues, homelessness, parental rights, gun control, overregulation, infrastructure failure, and the list goes on.

I realized that I was not just in way over my head (which I already knew), but I also didn't have a coach to guide me or my campaign through the minefield. We had a great consulting team in DC and a top-notch campaign team on the ground in California that included leaders from past campaigns. But I needed much more if I was going to have a shot at winning. The incumbent had over one million dollars sitting in the bank and the other Republicans running had been in the race much longer than I had. They were more well-known in the community, as well. I finally came to a place where I told the Lord that unless I could find that one person who could help me with the campaign, it did not make sense for me to continue running.

We had interviewed a few potential campaign managers, but none of them really fit the style of our campaign or had the experience necessary to run at the congressional level. I understood that running my campaign wasn't a very appealing job. We were asking someone to uproot their entire life on a whim and move to California to run a campaign for the most unlikely candidate.

Yet, in very God-like fashion, something we could have never planned took place. Through a conversation with a friend of mine in a hot tub in Oklahoma, I was connected to the former campaign manager for the governor of that state. His name was Aamon Moss.

Just a few years earlier, Aamon stood praying on the Great Wall of China with his friend Kevin Stitt. They were asking God how they could use their lives to impact the next generation. God spoke to them about running for political office and working to change the laws, landscape, and trajectory of culture. They came back from the trip and Kevin decided to run for governor of Oklahoma. He enlisted Aamon to manage his campaign. Neither of them had any political experience. Kevin was by far the biggest outsider, but he found a way through the twelve-person Republican primary to win in the top two. The final race was against the mayor of Oklahoma City and Kevin won a stunning upset to become the next governor. It was one of the biggest political surprises of the 2018 mid-term races.

Soon after our first meeting, the Lord clearly spoke to Aamon to move his family from Oklahoma to California and run my long-shot bid for Congress. We had a catch phrase that we coined the moment his feet landed in California. It was B.I.D. We did not want to run this race to blend in, play politics, or go with the flow. We wanted to Burn It Down. We were there to change the old systems, the old structures, the polarization, the division. The entire system was especially corrupt in California (on both sides of the table).

I liked Aamon immediately, and even more so after we came up with our catch phrase and agreed never to compromise on what we believed to appease anyone politically. Keeping our souls and integrity intact was far more important than winning a seat in Congress. We were not in the business to compromise. We were in it to B.I.D.

———

There were many obstacles to navigate in the final months of the race. Every day I would vacillate between feeling encouraged and feeling depressed and overwhelmed. I like to think of myself as an emotionally stable person, but the pace and demands of the campaign started to wear me down. My wife was also feeling the weight of campaign life. She worked hard to support me and the kids and was constantly gracious with my crazy schedule. I lived most of my days on the road either trying to keep our three non-profits afloat with conferences or hosting fundraisers and rallies for the campaign.

My ambitious goal was to raise $350,000 for the primary campaign and then ten times that amount for the general election. I knew there was no way to out-fundraise the current incumbent. I could, however, eclipse the other challengers and surprise the incumbent at just the right time. He had such deep pockets of wealth and massive backing in the Democratic Party. There was not even a chance I would catch up with him in the primary.

Every morning, I woke up with a heavy weight on my shoulders to fundraise and grind away for the cause. There was always way more to do than there were hours in the day. It was exhausting and hard to find a clear "win" because there was no measuring stick of productivity in politics. I thrive on finding ways to gauge and achieve success. There's no better feeling than going to sleep at night knowing I was able to accomplish what I set out to do that day. Campaigning was different. All I could think about at the end of every day were the things I didn't accomplish, things that could have given us an edge. It was a rat race—a never-ending cycle of "we can always do more."

Running for political office, with all its complications, can be simply broken down into the key business of selling yourself and selling your message. So out of all of the tasks our campaign team was taking on, there were only two things that I alone could do: talk to voters and raise money. I didn't mind the former, but I loathed the latter.

One summer during high school, I worked at a telemarketing agency selling magazine subscriptions. The pay was primarily based on commission, and I could make over $1,000 a week if I really set my mind to it. I hated it. I finally had to quit because it was just too painful. I cared too much about the people on the other end of the line. I always felt like I was scamming them out of their hard-earned money. I vowed to never do that type of job again.

I felt like I was back at that agency, doing the very thing I hated the most. I guess God has a sense of humor. Had I known all of this when I was on that plane flying home from DC with warm fuzzy feelings of excitement coursing through my veins, I would not have touched this congressional run with a hundred-foot pole.

———

Congressional districts consist of approximately 750,000 people. Some large cities and regions may have a little more and some rural areas may have slightly fewer. If you worked all day, every day at shaking hands, speaking at events, and hosting meet and greets, you wouldn't even meet one percent of the population across that district. The only way to reach everyone is through TV, radio, direct mail, and the internet. All of those mediums cost a significant amount of money and time.

Despite my displeasure and distaste for fundraising, I needed money to reach people with my message. Reaching out to every single person I had ever known to ask for money was humbling. The calls were difficult, at first, as I tried to dance around my purpose for calling (even though most people caught on early in the conversation). Then I started to get more direct as I went on and our financial needs became more critical. I finally got over the awkwardness and just went for it.

With every phone call, sharing my message with both friends and strangers, I started to believe my own message. I was also blown away by how much my platform of change, hope, and standing up for family resonated with people across America. I guess hope is a powerful thing. People I had never met before were moved by the risk and faith of our campaign. Many partnered with us and I was grateful for every dollar that rolled in.

We crunched the numbers to see how much we would need to raise daily to hit our goals. Each day, we would need $5,000 to reach $350,000 before the end of the primary. We would need to raise far more for the general election. And this was a cheap congressional race compared to others across the country. Campaigns in heavily contested districts can reach twenty to thirty million dollars!

Raising money became my main focus, and I needed to kill my pride and worries about my reputation in order to do it. There are many reasons why it is difficult for young people, Christians, and especially outsiders to run for public office. The financial aspect is one of the biggest hurdles to overcome. To quote the great Winston Churchill, "Politics is not a game, it's an earnest business."

Aside from fundraising, there were also the local, county, and state Republican Party chair members to win over. They had absolutely no idea what to do with me, and frequently told me so. I was a total wild card that threatened their perfect plan with their groomed candidates. Initially, they did not like me because I decided to run without asking their permission. It continued to get worse from there. Every time I visited their offices across the district, I was met with skepticism, suspicion, and disgust. They disliked that I lived outside the district I would represent (even though many past candidates had done that same thing). But they also did not like my long hair, my approach, or that I was a member of Bethel Church.

No one really took me seriously until I raised my first $150,000 and secured endorsements from well-known political figures. My strategy was completely different from anything that had been done before. I relied heavily on engaging the church and meeting younger voters wherever they were—outdoor parks, sporting events, or festivals.

Because the Republican Party chairs knew it would take me two to three hours to drive in for meetings in the district, they took advantage of that often. They scheduled last-minute meetings that they knew I could not possibly make. This gave my competitors the stage to share their platforms.

I had a complicated and jammed schedule each day that required the help of a full-time assistant. My days included fundraising calls, press engagements, travel to and from fundraisers and events, meetings with my non-profit staff, and being present for my family.

The committee members continued to recommend that I cut my hair almost every time we had an interaction. I was clear from the onset that the hair was not going anywhere. It was not so much about the hair but what it represented: my commitment to voters and the world—that I would not conform to the mob of political pressure. I know that sounds hilarious and mildly outrageous in the more "tolerant" culture we experience today, but it was a real issue in my campaign! They also did not believe that someone from the "church" could successfully run for a powerful political position. Ultimately, I refused to bow to their will and that is what drove them wild.

I was a little surprised by their behavior at first. I wasn't combative or attempting to stir up dissension. I actually thought they might be open to a fresh face in the party. The Republicans were on a twelve-year losing streak in district three. All of their past candidates looked and sounded very similar. The party had even dropped in ranking on the list of registered voters in California, falling behind Democrats and "No Party Preference." The definition of insanity is doing the same thing over and over again while expecting different results. Well, the Republican Party's approach in district three felt like insanity occurring right before my very eyes.

Because I did not fit the mold and bend to their every wish, the local Republican committee members didn't just refuse to support me; they actively fought, fundraised, and mobilized against me. They dissuaded people from joining our canvassing efforts across the district neighborhoods. They sent "secret spies" to the church events where I was speaking or leading in order to record everything that I said or sang, hoping I would slip up. They would capture video and pictures of my kids and harass my wife when she was with me. I was running on their platform, with their same policies and goals in mind, and still they worked against me.

From the moment we launched the campaign at the outdoor venue in Vacaville, we consistently held the largest political rallies of any candidate in that region in the previous decade. We were registering thousands of new voters and engaging a demographic that had been largely unreached. Yet the party I chose to stand with was vehemently against me.

There was also another candidate running who began spreading false and accusatory stories about me and Kate. They were not even remotely true. In fact, they were outright slanderous. Yet, my advisers and consultants urged me never to "punch low" and retaliate. That was the old school mob mentality of politics and I truly aspired to run a different kind of campaign. Even though it took everything inside of me not to lash back and defend myself, I remained silent. We kept pressing forward.

As the attacks from our own party increased, so did those from outside the party. Nearly every single day, we would get verbally abused and trolled online. We had to insert a statement on all social media channels advising everyone that we would block inflammatory and explicit comments. There were just too many of them to respond to and defend! The attacks were relentless, calling us everything from "white supremacists" to "false prophets" to a bunch of expletives I will not mention here. I knew that if we could not withstand this initial barrage of hate, then there would be no chance I would make it in the general election. That would be when the death threats, big tech censoring (Facebook, YouTube, and Google headquarters were right outside the district), and constant harassment would come.

———

The most painful resistance was not from the outside or from our own party, but it was from our friends. Many pulled away in silence and distance once I announced that I was running. I was naive to believe we could secure backing from many of our friends.

Although the political venture felt out of left field for many, it was not out of my character for us to rush in to face a crisis. Just as we mobilized a team to help refugees trapped by ISIS, or created a plan to rescue temple prostitutes caught in India, this was our attempt to confront the crisis eroding society in our backyard. I did not even like politics! We were just following the voice of the Lord as He called us to take a stand.

As the campaign sped forward, friends, leaders, and family withdrew from us. It happened quietly at first, but then became more apparent. Most people in my own record label turned the other way with what felt like more suspicion than support. It was the same with many good friends in our local community. It was painful—we thought so many of them knew our hearts and motives. We had taken so much time to explain and over-explain why we were doing what we were doing. We tried our hardest to bring people on the journey that led us into politics. Churches and ministries that did not agree with my political stances stopped inviting me like they had in the past. It was deflating as my worst fears materialized.

After being part of so many prayer meetings, hearing so many sermons, and singing so many songs about justice, righteousness, and truth prevailing, we were compelled to action. I came to the place where I could not attend another pro-life rally until I actually took a stand for the unborn through legislation. I would have run the entire race again and again just for the millions of babies aborted every year in America. I felt like I was becoming the fulfillment of those haunting prayers on the National Mall in DC that I prayed with tears as a teenager. I just didn't know it would come at such a cost or require such sacrifice.

I believed the Church had grown tremendously in championing people to bring the kingdom of God to the different sectors of society and culture. All except for one sector. We love sports heroes who throw the winning touchdown and say, "I just want to thank God" at the end of the interview. We love celebrities when they show compassion and even slightly hint at following Jesus. The same goes for billionaires who give extraordinary amounts of money to feed the hungry and eradicate disease around the world. We applaud them. But the moment a Christian—one of our very own—steps into the political arena, we do not know how to support them. It is too volatile and risky for our "politically correct" culture. It is far easier to try and stay out of it while proclaiming "politics are dirty." The Church easily becomes divided and does not know how to rally resources, support, or even prayer. The worst was when they would voice their support in private but then purposefully stay silent in public.

There were, however, many surprising relationships along the journey that God brought our way. New faces and new friends arrived from very diverse backgrounds who we may have never met if I hadn't chosen to run. There was a common synergy established as we all longed for the same thing: change in California!

These new friends surrounded us. They encouraged us. They prophesied over us. They befriended us. They canvassed entire neighborhoods with their family and friends for us. They donated themselves and their time and helped us fundraise. I am not sure how a season can be one of the most relationally traumatic and encouraging at the same time. That season fit both of those descriptions.

The flood of questions, comments, and perpetual invitations to defend ourselves over things we did or said was overwhelming. This was especially true after my visit to the White House and picture with the president. I could easily spend my entire day answering emails, phone calls, and social media replies and never reach the end of those questions or comments.

There is a story in the Old Testament that gave me insight and even solace in the last few months of the campaign. God had called us to a clear assignment and I had to learn how to get free of the noise so I could focus. It was the story of Nehemiah building the wall that felt most relatable to me. As he took up his call to rebuild, many people came to ask questions and offer their advice. Some of their questions were probably genuine concerns and those people felt they deserved an answer. But Nehemiah feared God more than man. He said, "Why should I come down from there to answer you when I am doing what I am called to do here on the wall?" (Nehemiah 6:3 paraphrase). This became my answer to many of the critics that I knew we could never appease.

———

The primary election in California is held on Super Tuesday—in this case, March 3, 2020. Our team was running a million miles per hour and every staff member was putting their whole heart into the campaign. I had raised just over $300,000—which I felt was pretty amazing! I hadn't quite reached my goal, but it was close. The fact that we convinced anyone that we could flip a seat in California felt like a miracle. I secured the endorsements of many acclaimed voices that could bring credibility to my campaign. Our national presence was growing. We were getting mentioned almost daily by major media outlets. Our social media accounts were gaining followers and we were one of the most followed congressional campaigns in the entire country. There was so much to be grateful for. It seemed like our hard work was going to pay off.

I started to feel a disconnect, however, between our platform nationally and our ability to reach the voters who would decide my fate locally. District three is one of the largest congressional districts in California and covers hundreds of square miles. When I wasn't traveling or raising money outside of California, I was traveling all over the district to host fundraisers and speak at churches, coffee shops, backyards and anywhere and everywhere people would have me. I hustled hard to overcome every obstacle in our way. But I was also running myself ragged.

Our entire game plan was dependent on millennials and churchgoers turning out in record numbers at the polls. I deeply desired for this to be one of those miraculous campaigns, where no one could really explain what happened when they looked back. I fully expected God to break in and prove to the skeptics, cynics, and haters of the world that we were actually called to do this. In the process of us being vindicated, only God would get all the glory for the victory. At least, that's how it looked in my mind.

The Sunday before the election, I spoke at three different churches across the region and emphatically and passionately pleaded for them to show up at the polls. I could hear the "amens" championing my message throughout each service, but I felt doubt creeping in, telling me they would not show up to vote.

A conversation that took place the month we launched the campaign came flooding back to my mind. I met with the last Republican to represent district three, twelve years prior. He didn't really like my long hair but quickly moved past that and realized maybe there was some value and energy in taking a fresh approach. He acknowledged he was likely out of touch with the current trends.

He asked about my strategy and I told him plainly, "I will use whatever influence I have in the Church to get them registered and to vote their values with me." I then said, "And we are going to reach out to millennials to get them connected to the power of their vote." He looked at me with a blank stare and then laughed. "Sean," he said, "if you want to hold a prayer meeting, then the church is a good place. But everyone knows in the political world that the Church does not vote! And I know that has not changed one bit since I left." He looked at me and spoke with complete seriousness, "You need a new strategy, man. Don't *ever* count on the Church to have your back."

———

The night of the election was full of every emotion you can imagine. It carried a weight of finality. I had put everything I had into my campaign. My heart had been invested ever since leaving that meeting in Washington, DC, even before I made the decision to run. After eight months, I was physically, emotionally, and spiritually spent.

I spent the next day fishing with my campaign manager. There was nothing more to do. Toward the end of the day, he looked at me and said,

"God's will is going to be done. So don't worry."

I did worry, however. During the three-hour drive to our campaign office, I shared with Kate how embarrassing and deflating it would be if I failed. I also listed the reasons I thought that was impossible—I had put in the hard work, raised the money, mobilized the Church, beat the streets with our message. It felt like we had momentum all around us.

The state of California has a unique primary system where all candidates from various parties run together and the top two candidates with the highest overall number of votes move on to the general election. That is why it is not uncommon to see two Democrats at the top of the ticket in various races. I knew it would be a sheer act of God for me to beat out the incumbent in this race, but I sure thought I would come in second place at least!

Losing was not an option. We had gained an army around us that felt like family. They had given everything to the race and I honestly just wanted to win and move on for their sake! I also wanted to win just to prove the haters wrong. It would bring validation to our decision and make us look good in the process. Who wouldn't want that? Last, I believed God would meet us in our place of risk and honor the work of our hands.

Instead, my worst fears were realized that night. As the votes came in, a room full of family, friends, and strangers were privy to one of the most deflating moments of my life. The cheers of victory never came. There was no sound of popping champagne bottles, no celebratory Instagram photos, no victory speech.

While the results were not final or official until the next morning, the writing was on the wall the moment the first county's tally rolled in. Defeat was thick in the air. My usual optimism disintegrated and I felt hollow. Within the first few minutes, I was in third place and behind by thousands of votes. With every new result, county by county, my fears were solidified.

The voices of everyone who had mocked and criticized us grew louder in my mind. The distance and absence of many of my friends became even more amplified. I had wasted eight long months of my life. It was hope deferred like I had rarely ever felt before.

I have never pretended to smile as much as I did that night as I said goodbye to all my supporters, friends, and staff. I even tried to hold myself together on the drive home. It was a quiet, lonely drive.

The next twenty-four hours were absolutely brutal. I didn't want to get out of bed the following morning. The last time I felt that way was when my dad passed away.

There was no silver lining here. Nothing brought me comfort or solace. I just felt utter failure, shame, and embarrassment. Not only that, but for the first time in a long time, I questioned my ability to hear God.

CHAPTER 17

THE BEGINNING AND THE END

There is a brokenness and humility that come with defeat. That election night failure broke me in more ways than one. I had sacrificed and risked so much to jump into something that I initially didn't even want to do. It would be one thing if the campaign had been a lifelong dream. I would have come out of the defeat even more motivated to try again. But I never had a dream in my life to run for Congress or even engage in politics.

My wife and I were exhausted and weepy all the following day. At one point she said, "I don't really know how to feel. I am so mad and so sad. But

I feel more angry because I know you did not even want to do this. I know this was never even your idea." She brought up the night I was given the prophetic word in the green room in Los Angeles and how she felt tricked by it. Hearing her verbalize that brought all those memories back for me.

Sure, it was embarrassing to lose. It was humiliating to face everyone who believed in me, prayed over me, and donated to the campaign. But that was not the main source of the ache in my heart. It was also not the shame from the skeptics, the cynics, and the trolls. I did, however, have to unplug from social media and texts for a while after the election. But I knew that I would overcome the failed expectations of my friends and family. I knew I could overcome the criticism from the peanut gallery.

My biggest battle, however, was with my understanding and faith in the promises of God over my life.

Out of all the ministries, seasons, initiatives, and adventures I had chased after in my life, running for political office was the one endeavor that included the clearest directive and word from God. He worked through dreams, visions, words, friends, maybe even angels and the whole host of heaven to convince me, over and over again, that He was with me. There wasn't a single close friend or advisor who told me to my face not to run. It seemed like the collective choir of our closest friends was all singing the same song over my life in that season: "This is the word of the Lord for you right now!"

That was why my wife was so angry. That was why I was so angry. The cost of the last few months on my life, my family, my marriage, my finances, my ministries, and my reputation felt irreparable. I was forever tainted by politics and there would be no escaping that in a politically correct culture. The damage felt heavy and unpredictable. What do I do with the promises from God that brought me this far? Since this was entirely His doing, where, when, and how would the redemption come?

I told people many times throughout the campaign that I never received personal confirmation from the Lord that I was going to win the congressional race. Others seemed to hear from God quite frequently that I was going to win. I had an entire folder on my computer that my staff created to collect and categorize the prophetic words, prayers, and visions people had during the campaign. I would often browse through them and feed my soul when things were rough or felt bleak. Now, however, I began to question every single one of those words. They had once brought me comfort, but now I only felt confusion.

———

After Super Tuesday, I decided the best thing for me to do was to shut out the noise, opinions, and suggestions from friends, family, and even my own campaign team. It was spring in Northern California and we had just entered a lockdown due to the explosion of COVID-19, a rapidly spreading coronavirus. I spent my days outside working on my property and processing with the Lord.

A few weeks later, a pastor from New York City emailed me a link to a message I had preached at her church the last Sunday of 2019. I normally never listen to past messages, but this pastor told me that her entire staff was listening to this word again and it was bringing them clarity, vision, and perspective for how to navigate the current global pandemic in their hard-hit city. I was intrigued.

During the message, I reference a rather obscure passage in the Bible I had never preached on before. The passage contains John's initial reaction to the prophetic vision God unleashed on him in Revelation chapter one. He was alone on the island of Patmos and was overcome with fear and anxiety after just a glimpse of God's vision. John described that moment in Revelation 1:17 (TPT): "When I saw him, I fell down at his feet as good as dead, but he laid his right hand on me and I heard his reassuring voice saying: *Don't yield to fear, I am the Beginning and I am the End.*"

The Lord spoke directly to John's fear and rebuked it. John had only received a glimpse of what lay ahead for the world. There were still twenty chapters ahead of intense and otherworldly revelations. John had no idea of the events that would pass before his eyes concerning the end of the age—images that could easily bring panic, fear, and discouragement.

Before he had a chance to panic, however, God reminded John that He is the Beginning and the End. The vision, John's life, all of eternity are His story and He alone is the one writing it. Because He is the "author and the finisher" (Hebrews 12:2) of our faith, we can trust that this story will always end up "for the good of those who love Him" (Romans 8:28).

God's gentle yet firm response to John's bewilderment and fear overwhelmed me. Tears ran down my face as I sat listening to my own message. That single scripture cut through my confusion and reminded me that it is not me but God who is writing my story. Hearing myself preach felt like looking over an old journal entry where you shared the testimony of God's goodness. You begin to remember His grace again.

The bigger story God was writing with my life came into focus. I have been through plenty of valleys of disappointment, despair, and hopelessness. But not once has He left me hanging in the process. Not one time did God ever fail to come through. He always turned every situation around to bring redemption, hope, and restoration. As recklessly as I had run after the prophetic word into the political arena, I wanted to run and discover His bigger purpose behind it all.

———

I took the following months quarantined in my home to take inventory of everything I was giving my life to. His faithfulness became the lens through which I viewed every last detail. I did not receive any immediate answers as to why things happened the way they did. Instead, I gained confidence that it was going to all make sense in the end. He is the author of my story.

I created a list that I called "The track record of His faithfulness." Once I starting writing, the list quickly grew longer and longer. I couldn't stop! This process brought perspective, but it also filled my heart with expectations for the things to come.

Iran is the last nation on my sticky note list that I wrote years ago. As I recalled God's faithfulness to make a way for me to visit the other four nations on the list, I experienced a wave of confidence that the fifth nation would be a piece of cake. He did not bring me this far to leave any promise unfulfilled.

"The track record of His faithfulness" anchored me throughout the turbulent days that the entire world was facing and still is facing even as I write this. The rapid spread of the COVID-19 virus and the devastating effect it is having on the elderly and immunocompromised have forced almost every nation on Earth into total lockdown. Just a few months before writing this, people were being instructed not to leave their homes unless it was an emergency. Schools were, and in many places still are, closed. Businesses are shut down. Churches can no longer meet.

Even now, we have nowhere to go nor the slightest idea of when it will all end. Our once booming economy is in a total free fall. The mainstream media is perpetuating a fear-based narrative that is propagating the worst-possible scenarios. Most people do not know any better and are buying into it, hook, line, and sinker. Panic and pandemonium are filling the hearts of the masses. Uncertainty and chaos are erupting in many nations as governments and world leaders struggle to grapple with the spread of the virus.

On top of all that, the Church is scattered. She is isolated and alone. The sound of her powerful corporate worship is silenced. The vacuum created by city and state ordinances prohibiting the Church to gather is giving room for fear and confusion. Many have forgotten the promises of God as they battle to simply survive each day.

Alcoholism and drug use seem to be at all-time highs. Many are concerned that the suicide rate may skyrocket. Anxiety and depression hang over the nation. As all of this unfolded, and still is unfolding, I began feeling so thankful that I did not have to continue running a congressional campaign through this crushing global pandemic. I could not imagine how I would afford a $30,000 per month payroll, while continuing to fundraise upwards of $3 million in a crashing and unstable economy. Millions of people have already lost their jobs and industries are experiencing irreversible damage. The last thing on people's minds is giving money to fund a campaign for an election six months away. Due to the lockdown, it is impossible to even host in-person events or fundraisers!

One incredible gift through all the madness is the time I have had with my family. Coming out of the most taxing season of my life, I was then stuck at home with my wife and four kids. It was such a massive blessing and we needed it more than I knew. We began to implement daily "adoration" times together as a family. We either turn on worship music or I pick up a guitar each morning and we all fix our eyes and hearts on Jesus. The kids color and draw whatever picture God is showing them. You would not believe the profound things my kids have created during this season! There is really no other answer for the current crisis and nothing else we could do. The presence of God has become our only option to wrap our home in peace.

The most powerful and sophisticated nation in the history of the world has been brought to its knees by a virus. The robust economy is imploding. As all of this began to take place, I could feel the call once again to raise up a new sound of worship to break off the fear and release hope to every heart. I began to see how the campaign had solidified my influence to speak into the political climate of the nation. My fear of losing my audience along with losing the election was never realized. In fact, my platform and audience only seemed to grow as people reached out to hear my thoughts on specific issues. People were listening.

Something else began to take place that deeply disturbed me and kept me up at night: the Church grew quiet in this season. Forced to shut down from the COVID-19 mandates placed upon houses of worship, the Church felt scattered and isolated. On top of all this, racial tensions are at an all-time high across America following the death of George Floyd by a crooked cop on the streets of Minneapolis. Protests and riots were taking place (and in some places still are), cities were burning, and people seemed angry, lost, and without hope. In the very hour where the world desperately needed leadership, hope, direction, and change, God's appointed "change agent" was in hiding and on mute.

Faith leaders have been afraid to speak up and speak out. It is not only the governmental restrictions that keep the Church from being present, but political correctness and the fear of "cancel culture" keep many leaders from declaring the truth of the gospel. Fear is driving the narrative instead of faith. Social media feeds have become a dumpster fire of hate, division, and "woke-ness." I could and can see many people drowning with no one to throw them a life raft. My wife and I also felt like we were drowning at times.

In a dream someone sent to us after the campaign, I yelled the phrase "HOLD THE LINE" to a massive group of people behind me while a vast army was forcefully advancing against us. This phrase really stuck with me and I could not get it out of my head. I believed it was a mandate for a new season in our lives after the campaign. In fact, maybe it was the entire reason why we did not win the campaign after all. In the midst of the chaos, confusion, and uncertainty, I knew we were called to raise a voice of courage, hope, and boldness across America.

In the midst of quarantines and unrest, I could see the Lord's heart for the Church, and "Hold the Line" became so much more than a phrase from a dream. I began to see it as a rallying cry for the body of Christ. A whole new vision unfolded as we processed the campaign, our lives, and what it would look like now to walk in brazen faith.

I invited my social media followers, friends, and the Church at large to join me and Hold the Line. The vision was to provoke believers across the nation to take a stand for what they believe in, as well as continue the momentum we had built during the congressional campaign. It would be a platform where faith, politics, and our family values would intersect to engage and bring real reformation. My calling to bring worship and prayer into difficult nations and impossible situations would be a core component of this movement. I desire to see the Church wake up from her slumber and truly become the LIGHT and the HOPE of the world!

A movement must be able to mobilize. With a phrase and a simple vision, I began traveling during the pandemic to the cities hardest hit with chaos and strife. Most people thought I was crazy. But we gathered the Church in St. Louis during a week of protesting, rioting, and chaos. Under the massive arch downtown, people actually showed up. Hundreds and hundreds of people! We prayed; we worshiped; we experienced racial reconciliation and healing. It was stunning and flew in the face of the current narrative dominating the mainstream media. Then I went to Minneapolis and we gathered in the same street corner where George Floyd died. God turned a place of trauma and hopelessness into a spring of life that night as hundreds more gathered! There were so many testimonies of salvations and healings, and we even baptized people that night!

The next week we gathered 400 worshipers on the Golden Gate Bridge in San Francisco a few days after the governor banned singing in church due to the virus. Orange County was next, then Los Angeles, New York City, New Jersey, and a gathering of over 5,000 on the beach in San Diego. A movement has now begun and only God knows where it is headed!

One of my favorite Billy Graham quotes sums up our vision for Hold the Line: "Courage is contagious. When a brave man takes a stand, the spines of others are often stiffened."

"The track record of His faithfulness" became a weapon to overcome the shame, disappointment, and confusion following the loss of the election. But it has also done far more than that. It planted my heart in a posture of overflowing gratitude. Feasting on God's faithfulness has become my sole aim. And from that place, He has given me the courage to continue taking a stand.

I know many people thought I was crazy for charging full steam into the campaign based on a word from the Lord. Many still do not understand our decision or even the tenacity in which we ran the race. That is totally fine. We are not accountable to the murmurs of the crowd. There is only one voice that matters in the end. There is only One we will ultimately be accountable to for how we steward our lives. His ways are not our ways. He calls us to do crazy things, even when we may feel we are at the precipice of our career, or when we feel most comfortable in the lives we have built. There is only One with the pen in hand, writing our story. It is a story so great that "You would not believe, even if you were told" (Habakkuk 1:5).

Through it all, the ups and downs, the losses and the victories, I understand more than ever that His story and His voice should be the defining goal of our lives. Whether you feel called to politics, entertainment, media, missions, or any other arena, if you learn anything from my story, let it be this: Follow the voice of God, no matter the cost.

Hasten now, my friends, and do not delay. There is still time to do what He has called you to do. There is still time to live a life of brazen faith.